Toujours Cricklewood?

Toujours Cricklewood?

Alan Coren

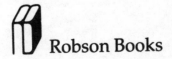 Robson Books

This Robson paperback edition first published in 1994
First published in Great Britain in 1993 by Robson Books Ltd,
Bolsover House, 5-6 Clipstone Street, London W1P 7EB

British Library Cataloguing in Publication Data
A catalogue record for this title is available from the British Library

ISBN 0 86051 869 8 (hbk)
ISBN 0 86051 941 4 (pbk)

Printed by The Guernsey Press Company Ltd.,
Guernsey, Channel Islands

INTRODUCTION *(fr. the Fr. **introduction**)*

Toujours Cricklewood? In other words, Not Cricklewood Again? I'm afraid so. Indeed, it all comes down to a matter of other words. Had BBC plans to adapt my earlier blockbuster *A Year in Cricklewood* for the tiny screen come to fruition, I should have earned so much money that I should never have needed to put processor to paper ever again. I should have left Cricklewood and gone to live in some toney tax-haven like Edgware, and neither bookshop-shelves nor you would have been forced to groan beneath this renewed burden on already crowded lives.

The unhappy fact of the matter is that the BBC, at the very height of complicated contractual negotiations involving not only me and my two agents, my three business managers, and my four accountants, but also Mr Robert Redford, Miss Sharon Stone, and a production unit of four hundred of the best professionals licence-money could buy, suddenly abandoned the entire enterprise. If this came as a bitter blow to everyone on the creative side, it was no less heartbreaking to thousands of ancillary workers in the fledgling Cricklewood tourist industry, in which I myself had no small commercial stake: everything, from Alan Coren's Cricklewood Sparkling Wine and Alan Coren's Cricklewood Fried Chicken to Alan Coren's Cricklewood Weekend Breaks and Alan Coren's Genuine Cricklewood Pine Furniture, will now, I fear, come to nothing.

God knows why the BBC suddenly changed its mind. It has been rumoured that someone in TV Centre took it into his head to wonder how on earth the witterings of a minor hack could be turned into a peak-time series with any hope of success, but personally I don't believe a word of it. I know the BBC pretty well, and that's not the way it thinks.

JUNE

The Green Hills of Cricklewood

You know how it is early in the morning, after you have done the thing with the toothbrush and the razor and you look out the window and it is not raining any more the way it was raining before it stopped, and there is just this mist coming off the sidewalk, now?

I squinted up at the sun which was making the mist do what mists do, and I thought: this is one of the days when you do not start work right away, this is one of the days when you walk up the street, past the old one who is bringing the milk and the young one who is carrying the mail and the tiny one who is pushing newspapers through those holes they have in the doors for pushing newspapers through, and you walk on up to where your street joins the big wide one called Finchley Road, because that is where the place is that is cleaning your trousers, and it is a good day to collect your trousers, before you start work.

But when I got to the big wide one, I noticed that something was not the way it had been before. I noticed this because I had to wait to cross to where the trousers were, on account of the big red buses and the heavy trucks that were driving between me and the place with the trousers and I knew it was not a good time to do the running with the traffic. You could get a wound, down there. These are things you learn. I remembered the time in Pamplona, when I was younger than I am now and had not learned those things, and a cab ran over my suitcase, and the suitcase was never the same, after that. So I waited, which was how I noticed what it was that wasn't the way it was before. There was a new café there, where there used to be a greengrocery.

The café was called Papa's.

When I finally crossed over to the place where the trousers were I said to the cleaning one: "I see there is a new café here."

"Yes," he said. "It has been here a week, now. They could not get this stain out. They have done a note. They say it is oil."

"They are right," I said. "It is the oil of the mower. If I ask for the Special Treatment they offer in the window, will it come out?"

The cleaning one shrugged. "Who can say?" he said.

I left the trousers with him anyway, and I crossed the road again, and I looked through the window into Papa's. It had a red tiled floor and round white marble-topped tables and black iron chairs and an electric fan in the ceiling, and I thought: I know why they have called it Papa's, and I went in and sat down.

A waitress came up. She was one of the slim ones, with the big dark eyes they have, if you are lucky.

"Welcome to Cricklewood," I said. It is the kind of thing you say, if you have known a lot of women, over the years. "It is good to see a café dedicated to Hemingway."

"I'm sorry?" she said.

I smiled. She was very young.

"The owner of this café would understand," I said, but gently. "Ernest Hemingway was a writer. He was one of the best writers there was. People called him Papa. He used to sit in cafés just like this, in the days before Paris was the way it is now. The cafés were called the Dome and Les Deux Magots and stuff like that, and they had red tiled floors, too, and white marble tables and black iron chairs and electric fans, and Papa would sit there writing in this ring-backed notebook he had, while the little saucers piled up in front of him."

"Does he still do it?" she said.

I looked away. I did not want to tell her it was thirty years since he had put the shotgun in his mouth.

"Ask your boss," I said. "He knows about all that."

She did the thing with the cloth that makes tables shine.

"My boss is my dad," she said. "That is why we called it Papa's."

I picked up the menu, after that. There were a lot of breakfasts on it.

"I'll have the one with the eggs and the bacon and the tomatoes," I said. "The Number Four."

"Is that the one with the fried bread as well?" she said.

"Yes," I said, "that is the one it is."

Salt in the Wound

I experienced a remarkable concatenation yesterday. I had gone to the Italian Driving School in Clerkenwell Road to make an enquiry on a friend's behalf (sensitively refraining from making any on my own, despite burning to know about the teaching of Italian driving, eg how to steer with your chin so that you can simultaneously keep the hooter depressed and leave both hands free, one to shake its fist, the other to raise its central finger), and when I came out again, I found myself a bit peckish, so I bought a packet of Smith's potato crisps.

I strolled on, thinking of nothing in particular, when I chanced to notice a blue plaque, high up on a redbrick wall at the corner of Hatton Garden, attesting to the curious fact that Sir Hiram Maxim (1840–1916), inventor of the machine-gun, had lived there.

That is the kind of information which suddenly makes one think of something in particular. While I already knew a bit about the great man – including the tragedy wherein a malicious Fate cruelly snatched him away in June, robbing him by only a few short days of the chance to see his greatest masterpiece, the First Battle of the Somme – I had no idea that this was where he had hung his hat. How tolerant landladies must have been, then! Not to mention the people in the flat downstairs; but, then again, you might think twice, might you not, before banging on the ceiling and thereby getting on the wrong side of a man who had just been practising at 500 rounds a minute?

These and similar woolgatherings having brought me to the end of the packet of crisps, I looked for a wastebin; and that I could not immediately spot one was what brought on the remarkable concatenation. I put the empty bag back in my pocket, where it remained until I got into the bus on Farringdon Road and dug for change. The bag was now in my hand again, where, by sheer chance, a word leapt off it and into my eye, the way this word, as I may have mentioned before, will. On the top right-hand corner of the packet, this legend ran: "Frank Smith sold Britain's first crisps to the pubs of Cricklewood. The salt-cellars he provided vanished as fast as the crisps. The little blue twist of salt was his ingenious solution."

Well I never. I mean, literally. Twenty years in Cricklewood, and I had never caught whiff nor whisper of our greatest son: for how else was one to describe a man who had invented not only the crisp, but also the little bag of salt to be a helpmeet for it? This was major genius. It was as if the Earl of Sandwich had come up with the pickled onion. Research was urgently called for. And when, an hour later, I rang Smiths (or as it now is, *eheu fugaces*, PepsiCo Foods International), one who still remembers the old days remembered them for me.

In 1920, Frank Smith was a young Cricklewood grocer, left to mind the shop while his employer holidayed in France. When the employer returned, he brought with him a wondrous tale of a little French restaurant where he had been served with thinly-sliced fried potatoes. He then got back to doing what employers do, leaving Frank to do what geniuses do. Geniuses have a bit of a think. After which, they remove their apron, politely hand in their notice, pop round to a bank manager whom they have circumspectly ensured never went short of a nice bit of gammon even in the darkest days of the recent hostilities, and buy the lease on a rundown Cricklewood garage which the instinct of genius tells them is just the place to begin manufacturing potato crisps.

How could it fail? It did not. The only commercial setback was that as Cricklewood's boozers fell upon Smith's delectable invention, they ungratefully nicked the saltpots he had loaned them. Smith, however, was up to that. Smith took fresh guard. The answer was in the bag.

I put the phone down, and dried my eyes, and drove to where the original garage used to be. It is now a B & Q superstore. I trekked its every wall, but there was nothing to show. What an odd world it is that reveres the machine-gun but not the crisp! Surely it is time to offer the honour of a small blue plaque? Preferably one with a twist in it.

Here We Go Round the Prickly Pear

I have nothing against poetry. If it were not for poetry, Postman Pat would have a black-and-white dog.

Poets, however, are another matter. While I derive much joy from what they do for a living, primarily because of the manner in which they do it, when they deploy this manner where it has no business, I derive no joy at all. I go up the wall. I kick things about. For, though I relish the ellipsis and elusiveness of poetry, though I am more than happy to tangle with the ambiguity, the obliqueness, even the downright inaccessibility which poets needs must bring to their tricky trade, I abhor their apparent inability to talk straight when straight talking is required. Never ask a poet what a spade is; you will be there all night.

Oo-er, I hear you murmur, something has clearly upset him today, he is normally the most equable of men. His wick must have something major on it. We are entitled to an explanation.

Let us go then, you and I, to the works of T.S. Eliot. Not to the wondrous conundrums of his verse, but to a letter he wrote, on 26 April 1911, to his cousin Eleanor Hinkley in Boston. He was 22, and on his first trip to Europe; he had gone to stay in Paris, but decided to nip over to London for a few days, and it is this visit about which he is writing. Here is the nub, both of his letter and of my complaint:

"I was out of doors most of the time. I made a pilgrimage to Cricklewood. 'Where is Cricklewood?' said an austere English-man at the hotel. I produced a map and pointed to the silent evidence that Cricklewood exists. He pondered. 'But why go to Cricklewood?' he flashed out at length. Here I was triumphant. 'There is no reason!' I said. He had no more to say. But he was relieved (I am sure) when he found out that I was American. He felt no longer responsible. But Cricklewood is mine. I discovered it. No-one will go there again. It is like the sunken town in the fairy story, that rose just every May-day eve, and only one man saw it."

Is it any wonder that as I stumbled upon that paragraph in my nice new *Letters of T.S. Eliot* yesterday I trembled with anticipation? Nor any less wonder that as I came to the end of that paragraph and found it was all that Eliot had to say about Cricklewood, I trembled, now, with rage? For God's sake, Tom, what did you *mean*? Why "pilgrimage" – what did you know beforehand? More to the point, what did you know afterwards?

Why is Cricklewood yours, what did you discover, why is it like the sunken town in the fairy story?

A terrible urge came on me to chuck the book in the bin; here was the century's greatest poet, certainly the greatest ever to fall for Cricklewood, offering me nothing of which I could make head or tail. Why could he not come right out and say what made my backyard so magical, so worth not merely a detour, but a pilgrimage? Why couldn't he have bunged Eleanor a simple postcard, *Here I am in fabulous Cricklewood, bloody ace, Guinness is tuppence a gallon, you never saw such big whelks, no bedbugs to speak of and I have to beat the women off with a stick, hoping this finds you as it leaves me, in the pink, T.S. Eliot?*

I did not, however, bin the book, I went instead to fetch another, for something had occurred to me; only two months after visiting Cricklewood, Eliot finished his first major work, *The Love Song of J. Alfred Prufrock.* Since he had fiddled and fussed with it for years, what might have spurred him, suddenly, past the post? I opened *Collected Poems.*

> Let us go, through certain half-
> deserted streets,
> The muttering retreats
> Of restless nights in one-night
> cheap hotels
> And sawdust restaurants with
> oyster shells:
> Streets that follow like a tedious
> argument
> Of insidious intent ...

I closed the book again. I had hitherto believed that the squalid, unnamed town in which J. Alfred murmured his glum monologue was part Baudelaire's Paris, part Dante's Hell. Now, I looked at his letter again. It was as I feared: how had I beguiled myself into believing he had said what I thought he had meant? Why had I imagined it contained one single word to suggest Eliot had actually *liked* Cricklewood?

Between the idea and the reality, falls the Shadow.

Strings Attached

I stand at the crossroads of those critical paths where concern meets interference, and I gnaw the indecisive knuckle. Call it the Cleveland conundrum.

Were the little boy at the upper window being assaulted, I should call the police, were he in physical distress, I should call an ambulance, were his premises burning, I should call the fire brigade; and were, moreover, any of these threats to his welfare on the point of getting out of hand, I like to think I should have no compunction in kicking down his door or shinning up his drainpipe, generally doing what I could to alleviate his misfortune. But none of these things is happening to him. All that is happening to him is that he is playing the violin.

Not that a stranger would know this. Were he to pass beneath the window, a stranger would think to himself: how odd that people in Cricklewood should not only keep a screech-owl but also allow it to dismember live weasels in the middle of the afternoon, funny old world, it takes all sorts, and amble on; but I am not a stranger, I have passed regularly beneath that window for two years now, and I know that what is being torn apart up there is Bach, and Gossec, and anyone else who, not content just to whistle fripperies in G major that came into his head during coffee breaks from serious composition, made the mistake of jotting them down. For without all those minuets and gavottes, thousands of tiny fiddlers would never get started, and thousands of parents would thus not entertain unrealisable dreams of the day when there would be a knock on the door and a little lad would ask if Tommy could come out to play the Bach Double Violin Concerto. Kids would not, in short, be jailed in summer bedrooms and forced to saw catgut in the service of some adult's crackpot hopes.

For there is nothing more surplus to this world's requirements than a bad violinist. Teach a kid bad piano, and he will nevertheless one day be able to make a fist, two fists, of "Knees Up Mother Brown" and be the life and soul of the Rat &

Cockle, teach him bad harmonica and he will raise the spirits of the forward trenches as the whizz-bangs fall, teach him a bad drum or cornet and he might well save the odd sinner, teach him bad guitar and he could find himself with ten platinum discs and three stately homes; but a fiddler has to be a virtuoso or he is nothing, unless of course he is Jack Benny or Jimmy Wheeler or Ted Ray, for whom bad violin was just another string to the comic bow.

It would probably not have occurred to me to address this theme, mind, if the kid were getting any better. But he is getting worse. He has been getting worse for two years. Every time I pass his house, fewer crotchets have managed to sort themselves into some sort of order. Give him two more years and he will be able to extrude nothing more from the woodwork than a single atonal shriek.

Worse, he is unhappy about this. Though I have often guessed him to be unhappy, it was only on Tuesday that I knew he was, because I saw him for the first time. He was standing at the window, holding the violin by the neck as if it were a tennis racquet, i.e. suggesting he was looking for something against which to splinter it. And when I smiled at him, I received in return not a smile but a bleak and pitiable shrug, after which he receded once more into the room and began rendering something even less recognisable than it was the last time.

What should I do? *De minimis non curat Childline*, nor will the council take into care every 10-year-old with two left thumbs, and I doubt that the Environmental Health Act can be deployed to suppress the noise of what, at an inspired guess, might have started life as Elgar's *Salut d'Amour* but has subsequently undergone variations so enigmatic that the neighbourhood's cats remain permanently on heat, but something must be done, if the kid is to be granted a normal life.

A letter to his parents? An anonymous phone call? A ring on their door to announce that my firm is always on the lookout for second-hand violins, best prices paid? I do not know. I know only that each time I pass the window, the sound I hear, however otherwise unidentifiable, is beyond any question a cry for help.

Which Way for the Gents?

You will recall – certainly if you have old Hackney Empire ticket-stubs among your souvenirs – that the great Billy Bennett used to describe himself as "Almost a Gentleman". It was his billing, and his act. I cannot clearly remember that act now, but foggily I remember it as being concerned with whelks, spats, aitches, and how to eructate in the company of Lady Mayoresses. He also had a funny walk, fashioned to indicate the legacy of several centuries of eugenic matrimony.

He was a big hit at the Empire. We fell about. Though we had no idea of what a gentleman was, the spectacle of what he patently wasn't brought the tear to the eye and embedded the helpless teeth in the stall in front. Forty years on, I can still taste the lacquer.

And forty years on, I am still no closer to knowing what a gentleman is, only to what he isn't. When, for example, poor old Trollope cries out in desperation: "I think the Duke of Omnium is a perfect gentleman. If he be not, then I am unable to describe one," what wobbles, willy-nilly, into my head is simply a vision of a more polished Billy Bennett, this time successfully controlling a knifeful of peas while managing to belch silently into an aspidistra without his monocle falling out.

Which brings me to trousers. Throughout my life, my trousers have never been gentlemen's. This, unlike many of the trousers, was perfectly fitting, in that throughout my life, I have never been a gentleman. What I have been is a gent, sometimes a proper one (ask any cabdriver), but above all a natty one, because gents' trousers is what I have always worn. And they have always been similar, even down to their names: they have been called Jax or Slix or Crux, and they have had a pocket on either side and one on the hip, and they have come with their own free belt in natty gents' hogskinette fastened by a buckle made of the kind of solid gold which doesn't come off provided you don't pick at it. That they were right for me was further indicated by labels which showed, in several colours, a gent like me walking about in them and looking flawlessly natty, sometimes with a dog. To remove this label, you had to gnaw at a plastic manacle until either it fell off, or your fillings fell out.

But last week was my birthday, and one of the presents my wife bought me was a pair of trousers. The first thing I saw when I unwrapped them was the label. It did not have a natty gent on it. It did not have a name with an x on it. It was not attached by a plastic hawser, but by a blue silken cord, and after I had untied it, I opened the tiny book which the label was and read that these trousers had been crafted by Gieves and Hawkes "to complement the wardrobe of an English Gentleman". At, moreover, Number 1 Savile Row, calling to mind the address of the Duke of Wellington at Number 1 London, and though I have always thought that a trifle vulgar, the Victorian equivalent of DOW 1 on the Roller, who am I, a mere gent, to say?

I looked at the trousers for some time. I may have trembled. Might it be that these were all that was required to make me, at last, a gentleman? I drew them on, and, yes, I entered a different world. That, however, I should not be able to remain there was immediately obvious: though they fitted perfectly at the waist and in the length, all the rest was, albeit very slightly, otherwise. For the gentleman, whatever he is, clearly has broader buttocks, longer thighs, shorter shins, thinner knees, plumper calves; these trousers may have been my size, but they were not my shape. Nor did they have a belt, and my own natty range would not fit the loops: what I needed to hold them up was, I imagine, an Old Etonian tie or, better yet, a hank of the silken rope from which a noble ancestor had dangled.

And what was I to do about the pockets? These trousers did not have three pockets, they had pockets everywhere; even the pockets had pockets. What for? Trout flies, snuff-boxes, monocles, foreign decorations, cartridges, heirlooms? How could I live up to them?

So I did a couple of Billy Bennett walks in front of the mirror, and took them off again, and they are back at Number 1 Savile Row now, being taken in, let out, all that. Who knows,

19

they may even stitch up a pocket or two to make me feel better, but it won't help. We all know that the main alteration will consist of shortening gentleman to gent.

JULY

Boot Hill

Dawn, the colour of a herring's belly. Grudgingly it rises, set-dressing the world for *film noir*. I know this period, I know this *mise-en-scène* I know this monochrome camerawork – bleak light trembling on puddled cobbles, sculpting hollows into gaunt faces, winking off this dented Hillman radiator and that battered Murphy radiogram (if I switched it on, would Albert Sandler pluck his Palm Court pizzicato at me, would Wynford Vaughan Thomas shout to make me hear him above the Berlin airlift, would Mrs Mopp enquire whether she could do me now?) – in fact, I know this very film, you must have seen *It Always Rains On Sunday*, John McCallum on the run, Googie Withers on the bed, the Mauser on the dressing-table, the East End on the scrap-heap?

Who could not recall it now, and here, on this drizzling contemporary sabbath in the vast Whitechapel yard behind The Blind Beggar, in which, 27 years ago almost to the very day, Ronnie Kray took out his own Mauser, because not much changes, nor that much, and blew the hapless George Cornell away? Resonances? Don't talk to me about resonances, the entire landscape twangs, and painfully, too: for here, nostalgia meets neuralgia, as if Proust had bitten his biscuit between busted teeth, and what resonates is poverty and villainy and decline and despair, it is the noise of beam-ends banging against one another, and aren't you glad you stumbled across this piece, do I or do I not know how to get your weekend off to a jolly start?

Let me dispirit you even further. What I am looking at behind The Blind Beggar is not, of course, a 1948 film, nor a 1966 assassination, but it could well be a 1993 air disaster: I am looking at a full acre of pitiful detritus, strewn clothes, broken dolls, dog-eared books, battered suitcases, ruined umbrellas; there are mounds of old shoes, heaps of old spectacles, piles of old hats; there are bits of clocks, and bits of tools, and bits of toys, and bits of cameras, and bits of almost everything that comes to bits. There is a box of dentures; another of hearing-aids. And slowly picking their way through all this heart-rending stuff, peering, fingering, muttering, sniffing, are hundreds of people. Looters, are they, transport officials, insurance assessors, loved ones, ghouls?

Happily, well relatively happily, none of these; nothing has come crashing down on Mile End Road, except the economy. What I am in fact looking at is London's largest boot sale, held here every weekend like so many others visited during my doleful research, but this one is the biggest and the best, ie, the biggest and the worst. Dozens of boots have trundled here today to disgorge their tons of junk, and with the creaking open of each newly arrived boot, something in the watching heart echoes that mournful groan, for the stuff disgorged is of such little worth as to be worth something only to (a) someone who would otherwise have nothing he could manage to buy, and (b) someone who would otherwise have nothing he could manage to sell.

True, boot sales also attract what might be called professional dealers, but only because professional is a pretty elastic term these days, and may be stretched far (and thin) enough to embrace not only those who have somehow come by a range of shopsoiled Tupperware basins at 50p each for the purpose of selling them at 60p, but also those who have somehow come by them at nothing at all for the purpose of selling them at anything they can get, preferably as quickly as possible, because one of the things they can get is their collar felt.

The majority, however, are neither professionals nor crooks but honest amateurs, selling from poverty to those who are buying from it. Here, for example, is a woman removing her little boy's scuffed shoes because she has haggled the asking price on a slightly larger scuffed pair down to a pound, and is throwing in his present ones in part-exchange. At the next stall, an old man is rummaging through a pile of 50p sink-taps, searching for one that turns easily; who can begin to imagine the domestic scenario that has brought him here? Behind me, I can hear a woman who has bought part of a mincer from one stallholder asking another stallholder if he has got the part hers hasn't, while a little further down the row, people are trying on second-hand glasses; God forgive me, I wait, for a minute or two, beside the second-hand denture box, just in case, but I move on, because even a hack has his shame.

I pause, propping my notebook against a grandfather clock with, poignantly, no clock, it is just a grandfather, and in that notebook my pen toys with the idea of *A Thatcherite Carol*, in which The Spirit of Free Enterprise Yet To Come (me) brings his night-capped victim (her) down to The Blind Beggar to watch Tiny Tim trying to flog his little crutch, but I soon cease pursuing this depressing line, because a bright side has occurred to me, and I wish to look on it.

For there is one, briefly, before it dulls itself. Because it is borne in upon me that, if we ignore for a moment the recessionary aspect of the hundreds of boot sales that these days dot the nation, there is no small pleasure to be had in the social archaeology they offer. Look at all these fat little cracked-Bakelite radios, their period logos, their reverberant names, Ferguson and Kolster-Brand and Sobell and Ekco, look at all these distressed cameras, Purma and Wrayflex and Reid & Sigrist, look at all these nib-buckled pens, Swan and Mentmore and Onoto and Conway-Stewart, look at all these wonky-lidded record-players, Dansette and Volmar and Melodeon, look at all these dismembered car bits, the Jowett grille, the Riley hub-cap, the Armstrong-Siddeley headlamp, all right, they may be stained, chipped, rusted, mildewed and generally clapped out, but they are the plangent reliquiae of post-war Britain, and the memory triggers, and the proud heart leaps.

Until, as I say, the bright side dulls, and it is borne in upon you that what you are really looking at are the plangent reliquiae of pre-post-industrial Britain: most of these names are stone-dead, these bits of junk are *memento mori*, they are at one with Nineveh, Tyre, and the Britain Can Make It Exhibition; for we cannot, apparently, make it any more, the legatees of all these boot-sold gew-gaws are Japanese and German and Korean and French and American. What we have here behind The Blind Beggar are the last battered knockings of the Industrial Revolution.

It is difficult, gazing across these serried ranks of rusty yawning boots and makeshift wooden trailers and little trolleyed stalls, to resist the conclusion that these might be the very handcarts the country is going to hell in. But for the moment, it is unsettling enough just to be reminded whence they have come. Look at that moth-swept old-clothes section! It is the 1960s: jiggle the rack, and they actually swing. Why, do you realise that, for less than a tenner, a man could kit himself out in authentic flares, foot-wide lapels, Cuban heels and a kipper tie, blow his 10p change on that hardly-scratched 45 of "Yesterday", and find himself never having it so good again?

Put Out More Flags

Patriotism is not enough. You also need planning permission.

Even if you are His Majesty King Taufa'shau Tupou IV, though in his case it doubtless went through on the nod. The latest Tonga-UK trade figures I have show that Tonga is a net annual importer to the tune of £850,000, and that is a catchy little tune, these days. The Borough of Barnet would not wish to muddy such waters. Nothing, furthermore, will persuade me that when His Majesty's triplicated planning application came in, the Borough of Barnet did not shriek, "Tell you what, let's treat this as a Friendly submission!", clutch the filing cabinets for support, and cackle till the tears ran down their cheeks. It can get pretty dull in Planning; you do not look gift horses in the mouth.

I know the application went through, because the flagpole went up, and the flag, moreover, went up it. Those of you who do not live just down the road from it may care to know that the Tongan flag is a truncated red cross on a rectangular white ground, and very nice, too, it adds a tone to Cricklewood that was not there before. It is there now because the Tongan High Commissioner, HE Mr Kipe, lives beneath the flag, in the official residence called Greenbanks, whence he drives forth behind the number plate 1 TON, which probably gave the DVLC a bit of a giggle, too, come to think of it, given that King Taufa'shau Tupou IV could put Helmut Kohl in his breast pocket and you'd never know he was there.

When the flag went up, I immediately, of course, remembered Mr Creswell. The Creswells lived next door to us when I was a small boy, and had a flagpole in their back garden. Many did, then. Every morning, before he strode forth to monger iron, Mr Creswell would run the union flag up his pole, every evening he would run it down again, and every St George's Day I would be invited in, as the relief bugler of the 1374 Cockfosters cub pack, to blow *Three Blind Mice*. It may not have accorded perfectly with the occasion, and, had I served at Balaclava, it might have gone a long way towards explaining the confusion, but it was all I'd learnt, and all, indeed, I intended to learn, if the Creswells couldn't do better than a rock cake and a glass of Tizer.

But more than even this sparked the synapses as the Tongan cross breasted the Cricklewood breeze. It occurred to me that a flagpole might sit well in my own backyard; beside the pond, perhaps . . . the splash of water, the croak of frog, the snap of pennant, the nocturnal thud of distant drum from some Wembley Stadium rockfest, a chap could think himself upriver, Mistah Kurtz, DC of Cricklewood . . . so I ran home and phoned Roberts & Perkins, mfrs of high-quality flagstaffs.

For a 20ft staff in timber, £140, they said, plus you'd need a tabernacle. Yes, I did ask, and it is what a flagpole gets bolted to, it is two 5ft lengths of 4x2, sunk to 2ft 6in and backfilled with concrete, make good, remove all rubbish from site, say £500 plus VAT, E & OE.

"Or?" I said, and they said, or there's fibre glass, no tabernacle required, plugs straight in, you could get out for £200, flag not included, do you want anti-vandal? Yes, I did ask, and the anti-vandal pole has its cords on the inside, so that members of the British Union of Fascists as skint as their heads can do no more than gnash their teeth at not being able to get their tattooed hands on a nice 6ft x 3ft banner worth, as I discovered from George Tutill of Chesham, £35.45, hand-sewn.

A bargain, for a patriot. So I rang the Borough of Barnet. You could hear breath being drawn in. For while a flag, no matter how large, does not need planning consent if flown from a flagpole on a roof, no matter how high, if it is flown from a flagpole on the ground, it needs all the planning consent it can get. Yes, I did ask, and they said yes, it did seem a bit peculiar, but there it was. Could take ages. Might never get it at all.

Which is precisely what swung it for me. I applied instantly. For a flag must stand for something, and while reasons for waving ours may be rather fewer than they were in Mr

Creswell's time, who will argue that British by-laws are not still the most remarkable in the world?

My Old Flame

A small part of me just died. You can get away with a line like that, in circumstances like these. Preferably it should be croaked, ideally through a week's stubble, and were I to be crouching in the dust and squinting up at a noonday gong of sun, that wouldn't hurt, either. On the second take, the director might even ask me to spit, since we are talking here about the days before tough guys cried, when the only water permitted to come out of a man's face at moments of profound emotion was saliva.

I have lost my Zippo. This is not a Marx brother or a Bulgarian van or a one-step furniture polish, it is a cigarette lighter. It is *the* cigarette lighter. It is the Platonic essence of cigarette lighters, of which all others are but flashy and inferior derivatives. Direct heir to the tinder-box, the Zippo is a plain steel oblong, two inches by one inch, containing a wheel, a flint and a wick-bound wad of petrol-soaked lint.

It does not have spring-loaded ignition, it does not have an electronic spark, it does not run on gas or titchy solar batteries, it does not have an adjustable flame or instant flint-load or valve-controlled fuel injection, or any of the other ritzy accoutrements of what modern marketing no doubt calls in-pocket personal enflaming systems; what you do with a Zippo is you thumb the lid open and then bring the thumb back across the wheel, and a flame explodes on the wick. It is a big flame, a man's flame, because you have to keep a Zippo topped up at all times, given its tendency to evaporate into surrounding clothing. This is not a shortcoming, it is the means by which Zippophiliacs recognise one another as soon as they enter a room; the twitch of the nostril is what we have instead of a masonic handshake. If there is danger involved in this spillage, so much the better, for we are hard men, unafraid to walk with risk, and while it has long been my conjecture that cases of so-called spontaneous combustion are in truth but Death serving notice on Zippo-carriers not to stand too close to open fires, frankly I have never given a damn in 30 years.

The Zippo cost me a thousand bucks in 1962, when a dollar was a dollar. Though I could have walked into a store and bought one for $5, that is not what I did; I bought mine with a year's worth of S & H Green Stamps, making the receipt of it a total Stateside experience, because it was not only a Zippo, as quintessentially American as the Coke bottle and the Cadillac fin, it was a metonymic signifier of all I had literally become: for a year I had stuffed my frame with frankfurters and chilli beans and buttermilk and toasted pecans and Napa Valley wine and Pilsbury cookies and Hershey bars and Grape Nuts, and everything else my local supermarket insisted I buy before they gave me the stamps, which meant that the arrival, at last, of the Zippo was nothing less than a triumph of symbiosis.

But it was also much more. It was a ticket to myth. Up until then I had been lighting my Chesterfields with a poncey little Ronson brought with me from England, but now I had a big butch Zippo, you could fire it double-action (cock it open, pause, flick, light) or fan it, single-action, with your thumb, this was the Zippo 45, the smokemaker, the lighter that won the West, this was the best thing a man could carry without a licence, it was what stretcher-bearers reached for to light last cigarettes on Iwo Jima, or at least on Iwo Hollywood, it was what limelighted Lauren Bacall's face just before the Hays Office drew the blinds and Phillip Marlowe's just before the blackjack met his ear, it was what you slid along the bar to the weepy torch-singer when it was quarter-to-three and there was no-one in the place except you and she.

Even in Cricklewood. For icons, like space-probes, go on emitting their signals forever, no matter how distant their source. Which is why, prime among my regrets about the Zippo's loss, is my regret for the manner of it: I should not have minded quite so much had I lost it in a poker game, or dropped it vaulting the Sing Sing wall, or left it on Lana Turner's bedside table, or even had it looted from my corpse by a German sniper. But I rather think it fell out of my pocket on the 13 bus.

Up Before the Beaks

One for sorrow, two for joy, 17 for a real pain in the neck. Hang on, 18. The lawn looks like nothing so much as the foyer of the Old Bailey, a mob of paunchy barristers in *sub fusc* waddling about and cackling deafeningly at one another in a language none but they can comprehend.

It is the cackling that is the worst. That they are also gobbling everything in sight is of smaller concern, because that is nature's way, man was not put here for the purpose of running outside every minute to protect each berry and insect, there is a pecking order, and if you didn't want to be a worm, you shouldn't have joined.

But the cackling impinges directly upon me. The cackling is the frontier at which man and magpie clash. It brings the magpies into my bedroom. At, for they know the one about early birds, 6.30 a.m. And I did not shell out good money on an alarm clock to be woken up an hour earlier by squadrons of *Pica pica* scrambling for a dawn sortie and so refusing to maintain radio silence that the mullions rattle. *Pica pica*, by the way, is not an old Edmundo Ros favourite, it is the name ornithology has given to the magpie, and if you look it up in the *OED* you will discover that it means a pathological craving for peculiar food. I do not need to look it up. I need only to look out of the window, because among those who are not drilling the lawn is one which is maniacally attempting to plier a wall-nail from the fence and another which appears to be going six rounds with the watering can.

This cannot continue, I said to myself this morning, and reached for the phone-book. I could not find the Royal Society for the Extermination of Birds (fashionable wimpiness has doubtless driven it ex-directory), but there was a number for one which regally protects them, so I rang it. After all, while the last thing I wanted was to protect them, that was the first thing the RSPB wanted, and if they knew I was about to run amok with a cleaver, they might well intervene with some kind of compromise. David Owen, say, might have a free moment.

I was not wrong. "Yes," said the RSPB, "there are abnormally large numbers about. Of course, the magpie is not a protected species, but I imagine you don't want to shoot them," (there you have it, some people have imagination, some don't) "so what we advise is that you make a cardboard cut-out of a bird of prey and put it on a pole in the garden. That often discourages them."

"What kind of bird of prey?" I said.

"We tend to recommend the kite," she replied.

I thanked her, and went to find *The Observer Book of Birds*. It said that the kite was now found only in Wales. Nothing about Cricklewood. There was clearly no point in nailing up a magpie-killer if the magpies did not know that that was what it was. It was not, after all, going to show what it was by killing any of them. Cardboard doesn't do that.

I flipped through the book. The shag looked really horrible. Sadly, it craves only fish. If I had a lawnful of herrings I would be on to a winner with the shag, but that is not what I have. I flipped on. It would have to be a kestrel. The kestrel lives everywhere. Unfortunately, it preys only on small birds, because it is never more than 13in high, but I was up to that. I would make it twice the size. It would be the biggest kestrel the magpies had ever seen. They would all have cardiac infarcts on the spot.

The largest cardboard I had was a carton which had once contained a radiator, the only paint I had ("slate grey head, chestnut back," said the book) was water-colour. This immediately soaked into the cardboard. I now had a giant beige kestrel with "DIMPLEX" written on its body, in red. Never mind: how literate could a magpie be?

So I went outside with the kestrel behind my back and I shouted so that the birds would fly off and not twig what was up, and I stuck the kestrel in the middle of the garden, and I ran back inside to watch and wait, and sure enough, it made a tremendous impact on the magpies.

Even as I write, there are four of them slashing away at it. Only "PLEX" is left. In ten more minutes, they'll have eaten the lot.

The Queen, My Lord, is Quite Herself, I Fear

The only time I lunched with the Queen, the first words she said to me were, "Have you any idea what a trial it is to own a golf course?"

I do not remember what I mumbled, but I do remember reflecting that when it came to pre-emptive strikes, my sovereign left Admiral Yamamoto at the post. I had turned up at her palace with my conversational fleet dressed overall, there was not a potential topic I had not buffed to shimmering nick, there was not a drollery unprimed, but she had dived on me out of the sun, and her first wave had devastated me; my battleships were going down by the stern, my carriers were ablaze, and where my submarines had once lurked there were now but pitiable patches of flotsam-dotted oil.

She then launched, while the prawn hung trembling on my fork, into a hilarious account of the shenanigans at her Windsor links, where a demarcation dispute between groundsmen and gardeners had left the fairways unmown. When she had finished, she asked my advice as to her best course of action. I put the prawn down and mumbled something else, drawn this time from my vast experience of owning golf courses, whereupon she said. "Was there an exact date when workmen stopped wearing boots? You never see boots on workmen any more."

The whole of, let us call it our conversation, followed this bizarre unpattern, the monarch unfalteringly displaying a surreal penchant so relentlessly nimble it left the clodhopper winded. It was like going ten rounds against a class flyweight trained by René Magritte and managed by P.G. Wodehouse. By the end of three hours, I had pledged my life to her. Here was wackiness of an order so incomparable it must have been hers by divine right. She was barking regal.

Her husband? I had first met him some years before, when as Rector of St Andrews I attended the investiture of Magnus Magnusson as Rector of Edinburgh, where Prince Philip was Chancellor. We were all in the robing room, struggling into our floor-length velvet numbers, when the Consort suddenly cried: "If we were stark naked under these, nobody would be any the wiser!" He then laughed for a very long time.

It thus came as no surprise to me when, soon after, their son stopped doing Bluebottle impressions and began confiding in flora, leaving me with a conviction rendered all the more unshakeable by the Princess Royal, who when I invited her to a *Punch* lunch and apologised for limping on a swollen knee, said: "Yes, it's been a ghastly year for equine VD. Did you know it can cause rheumatoid arthritis in jockeys? Everyone's taking phenylbutazone."

What am I trying to tell you here? Merely that I have been growing daily more irritated by demands for the Royal Family to shape up, remember who they are, and behave accordingly, because my view is that is precisely what they are doing. They are a very odd lot, and they stand in a long and remarkably impressive line of highly peculiar figures of whom this country ought never to cease for one instant to be proud.

Hitherto, we have cherished them for this astonishing distinction, Edward II, Richard III, Henry VIII, Elizabeth I, Charles II, George III and IV, Edward VII and VIII – and I pick only the royal tree's fruitier plums, the ones we relish most for their egregious lusts and vagaries and misdemeanours, for even the dullest have had their moments, be it George V's terminal injunction to bugger Bognor, or that exercise of Victoria's remarkable libido which, indulging itself at Windsor, could rattle windows in Cardiff.

So why are we distressed now at what delighted us before? Whence this nonsense requiring the current lot to be moral exemplars and behavioural models, because if they won't, then it is all up with them? They have never been anything of the sort; what they have been is a collection of flaky English eccentrics beyond the dreams of Ealing Studios, as thankfully unlike their subjects as it is possible to be. Oh, yes, we may rightly tremble at the thought that we might find ourselves married to one, but candidates have had a thousand years to be warned, and if in doubt, Sellar and Yeatman are a quick and easy read.

AUGUST

White Man Shriek at Forked Tongue

U p betimes this morning, thanks to the Provençal sun currently being so hot so early that the crack of a warping shutter puts a warning meteorological shot across your bows at around 7 am, I immediately discovered the need to sort out some serious wood-abuse of my own. For *gueule de bois* is what the French call a hangover, and mine was oaken; unable even to bid my wife good morning, I hobbled into the bathroom, filled the tub with cold water, and fell in.

Slowly, hygroscopy worked its little miracles: blood pumped, nerves twitched, joints eased, brain cleared, eyes opened. And it was all pretty good, until that last bit. That last bit was very bad. It was so bad that the eyes shut again. Each now had an image on the inner lid. The cleared brain said, "Tell me it is only a pair of tights or a piece of rope," but the eyes weren't having any. They knew what they knew. They opened again, and the brain threw in the sponge. It knew too.

It was not as if it hadn't been warned. For the past few days, the local media had exercised themselves over little else: thanks to the mild spring, the snakes had bred in unprecedented

39

millions, and thanks to the broiling summer, they were as unprecedentedly getting out and about. Because it is so hot, they like basking in the sun. We must not walk through grass in bare feet or open sandals. Fine. But because it is so hot, they also like not basking in the sun. Sometimes they like basking in the shade. You never know where you are with snakes.

Except when you are in the bath, when you know exactly where you are with them. Cut off from the door. Since I could now open my *gueule*, I debated calling out to my wife, but I did not know whether snakes had ears, and what they might do if they heard anything with them to which exception might be taken. I realised, indeed, how little I knew about snakes generally; I did not even know if they jumped into baths.

The sole reassurance offered by the French media was that snakes were more afraid of me than I was of them, but who would believe that? Why would it be afraid of me? Did it think I was going to slither out of the bath and sink my fangs into it? Was it terrified of ending up in some intensive care unit? Was it worried how its dependants would get its coffin back to England, never mind all the paperwork?

If it was afraid of me, it was putting a pretty relaxed face on things.

It lay by the wall, coiled like a Danish pastry, rubbing its head on the tiles and doing that thing with its tongue that you really don't want to watch it doing for too long. When I finally called out, it didn't react. At least, I couldn't see it react. It might have been thinking, "Hallo, there is something here more afraid of me than I am of it."

Why is there never a mongoose around when you need one?

So my wife, a model of *sang froid* when it comes to being on the other side of the door from a snake, phoned *le mairie*, who have an emergency line. I heard nattering, giggling, the sort of jolly exchange that makes you feel ten times more isolated than ever, and then she called out: "Could it be an *orvet* or a *couleuvre?*"

I explained briefly what I knew about snakes, hardly shrieking at all.

She fetched a dictionary.

"They want to know if it could be a slow-worm or grass-snake."

I again explained, even more briefly, what I knew about snakes.

"They say they are very pressed, and won't come out if it's harmless, which 99 per cent are," she called. "What do you want me to do?"

I glanced at what could have been the 1 per cent. "I want you to look up cobra in the bloody dictionary," I shouted, "and get them round here NOW! If you can't find cobra, try mamba."

There was more nattering after that, and more giggling, and she rang off, and said that what I had to do was soak a bathtowel until it was really heavy, then chuck it over the snake, run out of the room and slam the door, and they would come round and deal with it.

So that is what I did, and that is also why I am typing this, because it is the only way I know to stop my hands trembling. The *serpentiers* haven't arrived yet, but even if it turns out to be an overweight earthworm, I promise you I have no intention of letting them faze me. I just keep telling myself they're more afraid of me than I am of them.

Adventures in the Skin Trade

To gentlemen in England now abed, the nub of this whole tacky business is doubtless the possibility that it may well have given a terminal shake to the foundations of the House of Windsor; but let me tell them that, up here at the shellshocked Rivieran front, many another hitherto sturdy edifice is wincing as its bright stucco cracks and the Provençal tiles slide from its roof. For this time, it is we out here who think ourselves accurs'd, especially if we do not hold our manhoods cheap.

Or, indeed, hold them at all.

Now, my own current premises lie just a few miles along the azure coast from, if I may be permitted to switch Elizabethans, those topless towers where sweet Fergie was recently making herself immortal with a kiss, and while they may not be quite as swish as those which attracted the attention of the *Daily Mirror*'s property correspondent, they do boast a delightful swimming pool surrounded by comfy loungers which – though a brace of fleshy rompers might find themselves sinking slowly groundwards to the accompaniment of a somewhat unromantic hiss – are more than adequate for the solo sunbather. Furthermore, the spot is secluded by oleander and bougainvillea, and the nearest houses lie half a mile away, across the valley.

And now, a word or two about breakfast. Every morning, exemplary host that I am, I leap up as the first cicada salutes the rising sun, and run down to the village to buy croissants for the still-snoring household. English guests all, they cry that that is one of the great things about France, mmm, fresh croissants, mmm, delicious . . . they then nibble a corner, scattering the rest into a thousand flakes which float down so that a million waiting ants, having formed fours in the garden in anticipation of a scent on the breeze, may begin marching into the house with the unnerving precision of the Waffen SS, thereby giving me the opportunity to spend much of the rest of the day fruitfully engaged with aerosol and dustpan instead of frittering it away by the pool.

I do not mind this at all, because of the two joyous bonuses which go with croissant-fetching. The first is that I am early enough to get my hands on one of the handful of English newspapers which dawn brings to our local shop, and the second is that I can get back home in time not only to have my morning swim but thereafter to dry off on a floating li-lo, reading the paper before the mob have had the chance to reduce it to a tattered wodge made illegible by a combination of sun-oil and the dismembered parts of large swatted things which seem always to have their clogs popped in the middle of particularly crucial paragraphs.

And moreover, the most exquisite element of all is that the swim is nude. I do not intend to bang on anent the components of that exquisiteness, but I would just say that it is not exclusively sensual: pottering naked through dawn-dappled water not only puts the swimmer in pantheistic touch with darting lizard and rising lark, it allows him an atavistic glimpse of that brief pre-lapsarian time before the snake slithered down the tree and brought bathing trunks into the world.

At least, it did until last Monday. Last Monday, I hurried home with croissants and *The Sunday Times*, stripped off, hurled myself into the pool, and duly emerged to lie supine on the air bed and relish the news from home. And where would the expatriate first turn for this but to the "News Review" section? And where but there would he see two photographs demonstrating what may be done with what the caption described as an 800mm lens with a 2x converter?

And what would he do then?

He would immediately put *The Sunday Times* to a use for which it was not primarily designed. For by turning his head a fraction, he could see the hill-top houses half a mile away, and suddenly half a mile was a very short distance indeed. And who could say where Daniel Angeli might be today, telephoto in one hand, cellphone in the other? I cannot of course estimate my value, my line to the throne is somewhat tenuous, but every man has his price, and who can be sure that a great professional like Signor Angeli would turn his nose up at ten bob from the *Cricklewood Weekly Advertiser?*

So What's Eating You?

We are talking neither English nor French, though the passing eavesdropper might think we were talking both. What we are in fact talking is Navaho. Possibly Cherokee.

He says: "Was it Big Green Blobs Like Eyes But Not Eyes?"

I say: "No it was Red Waving Stalky Things."

He nods, and muses, and says: "Wings With Black Dots?"

I shake my head and say: "Wings With Orange Flecks."

Thus it is when non-entomologists meet, and thus it must have been when American Indians, having words but no nomenclature, first found their skin being punctured by horrible bugs and ran around yelling until someone asked them what it was they were yelling about. That is how so many of them ended up being called Bitten By Green Blobs and Dances with Stings and so on. At a guess.

And guesswork is the procedure, here in Dr Brocard's surgery, whither I have hobbled on one leg which looks like a leg and one leg which looks like a bag of rugby balls; for while he has some English and I have some French, neither of us has enough of either to identify what it was that sank its arsenal into my calf yesterday, so we have to proceed by a sort of verbal identikit.

Nevertheless, we do finally converge, thanks to my having got a good look at my attacker: four centimetres long, six green Anglepoise legs, feathery red antennae, orange polka-dotted wings, and somewhere hidden in all that extravagant and misleading frippery, like a Borgia stiletto concealed in a hand-tooled psalter, a poisoned hypodermic capable of inflating a human leg to twice its normal size.

I got a good look at it only because it was good to look at. It landed on my knee yesterday as I lay supine on the poolside grass, and as I watched it mince delicately about my shin, I felt that fashionable oneness which yokes us all together, large and small, upon this teeming planet, I felt that proper reverence at

God's niftiness with blueprint and spanner, and I felt that warm glow which suffuses us when a dumb animal seems happy in our company.

I say feel, but I did not know what feeling was until a good half-minute had passed, when it transpired that the thing was not ambling about just because it liked me or because it wished to prance its finery, it was looking for a decent picnic spot, which it finally found halfway across my left calf.

I know that that was what it was after, i.e. lunching rather than stinging, because when I stopped shrieking for long enough to swipe it from my calf, it left there a hollow proboscis full of blood. So I shrieked a bit more and sloshed on some stuff from the trunkload of unguents we had carted down to Provence for just such an emergency, but when I woke up this morning I realised that this hadn't been just such an emergency, because there was a bag of rugby balls in bed with me, proving that the unguent was a fat lot of use.

Not as fat a lot, mind, as the leg itself. But it is deflating now, thanks to Dr Brocard's having stuck his own equally painful needle into me to tap off a bathful of water, and while I am lying here on his bunk digesting a handful of antihistamine pills, it occurs to me that there could well be a book in this, because of all the wonderful books thrown together by Englishmen in Provence, none of them tells you what to swat.

English swatting is easy, we have only the wasp and the gnat and they both look horrible, even foreigners know where they are with these, but down here there are a thousand different nasties and very few of them look it, most of them look as though Fabergé were still in business, and you do not want to start lashing or aerosoling lest you expunge something as good as it is beautiful, which you do not discover it isn't until it has taken a lump out of you.

So I shall spend the rest of my holiday asking locals about Big Green Blobs Like Eyes But Not Eyes, and so forth, and I shall compile a comprehensive hit-list, and then I shall come home and find a publisher smart enough to agree that the optimum format would be a large, thin, flexible paperback with a wipe-clean laminated cover. With something like that, you wouldn't have to be Peter Mayle to make a killing.

Watching Brief

I am sitting here, at the prime corner table of the Café du Midi, sipping my second *double espresse* of the very early morning and watching the Provençal sun rise behind the little crenellated turret of the *mairie* across the village square, and it is not altogether unpleasant, listening to far cocks crowing and near bees humming, as the shopkeepers' hoses sluice the pavement and cyclists wobble through the spray on their way to work I do not have to do. And I am even happier that I have arrived early enough to bag the prime corner table, because Susan Hayward and Dana Andrews are here beside me, and I shall be able to spot everyone else making for the Café du Midi as soon as they turn the corner.

That is an important factor, if you are trying to get rid of Susan Hayward or Dana Andrews.

I have been trying to get rid of them for three days now. They are both in a little oblong box, whither they were convened for the purpose of sharing a rather superior weepie in which Dana nosedives his bomber into the ground, leaving Susan to bring up their illegitimate daughter by entering into a doomed *mariage de convenance*, ie hitting the sauce, sleeping around, sobbing a lot, ultimately losing the long-suffering jerk prepared to give her hapless by-blow a surname, and generally having the sort of rough time women had to have in 1951 if they were going to be able to expiate the fearful Hollywood sin of pre-marital nookie

46

and leave a thousand Odeons sniffling as the ubiquitous theme-tune rose in an irresistibly poignant crescendo. Not a bad tune, as a matter of fact, in this case: for though the lyrics of the eponymous *My Foolish Heart* would instantly bring the most arthritic set of toes to squirming life, the melody has lingered on for 40 years, and may still be found issuing from the better class of saxophone wherever jazz buffs foregather, mucked about of course yet sturdy enough withal to stir nostalgic stumps.

And if all that sounded like a sales-pitch, forgive me; when you have been trying to offload a turkey for three whole days, huckstering enters the soul. For the Café du Midi is where English expatriates, both permanent and tourist, congregate to trade videos; because despite foolishly declared intentions to spend the untanning evenings in finally mopping up Proust or attending *al fresco* Vivaldi recitals or even watching domestic television to, of course, improve their French (an unlikely result, given that it consists mainly of gameshows involving nerds shrieking inexplicable argot, academic discussions involving nerds shrieking inexplicable jargon, or dubbed American soaps where the anglophone viewer becomes transfixed by the attempt to read lips), everyone down here finally succumbs to buying a VCR and swapping tapes either brought or sent from the old country.

Now, usually, I have good stuff to trade, particularly with the permanent lot whose absentee tongues hang out for *Jeeves and Wooster* or *Morse* or anything else of a superior note, especially when it contains the added boon of country piles, straw boaters, Oxford colleges, unofficial English roses, and all the other resonant gubbins likely to implore the passing tribute of an expatriate sigh. But this trip, pressed for packing time, I grabbed the first cassette that came to hand, and though I have been hawking it hard, nobody wants it. Day after day I trudge down here to the Café du Midi and set out my meagre stall, I simper fetchingly at the gathering crocodile like a clapped-out tart in a Reeperbahn window, but they will not be fetched.

It is most dispiriting. I watch all the others gleefully swopping, say, *Singin' in the Rain* for a 3-hour compendium of *LA Law*, I hear them calling 'Anyone for six *Roseannes*?' and see the Oval Test waved in eager response, but the closest I have ever come to a deal was a woman with an *Eldorado* anthology which I should, God help me, gladly have taken off her had another soaphead not come by and stuck a swatch of *EastEnders* under her nose. And perhaps the worst part of it all is having to come home yet again to a hungry family lined up crying, 'What have you brought us, Daddy Bunting?' Only to have to shake my head and toss Susan and Dana back on their lonely shelf.

The Princess and the Pee

Dear Princess Anne, May I, on behalf of my good lady and myself, thank you very much for welcoming us aboard your hovercraft last evening? I realise of course that you did not do this personally, the welcome had been graciously vouchsafed to one of your stewardesses-in-waiting, but we appreciate that you are only human, you cannot be everywhere at once, and Calais Hoverport is a dead end at the best of times.

As a matter of fact, it had actually been vouchsafed to one of your tape-recorders-in-waiting, we could hear the crackle, but it is the thought that counts, though, if you will graciously forgive me, we did think it a bit naff not having a human being saying: "Welcome aboard the Princess Anne," especially as the thing was packed to the gunwales with foreigners; it does not exactly create the impression of a stylish maritime nation, it looks as though someone is trying to save a few bob; it even crossed my mind that there might not be a crew at all, just a long cable and a bloke in Dover with a big winch.

I don't know if you get down to your namesake at all, what with Save the Children and Bafta and being colonel-in-chief of the 8th Canadian Hussars and everything, there are just so many hours in the day, but dare I crave your gracious indulgence to suggest that it might not be a bad idea? It is, after all, hovering in your name, and while thousands of travellers acknowledge your gracious sense of humour in allowing something so, let's face it, daft-looking, to bob about under your nominal auspices, not a few also wonder how far you keep apprised of current conditions. Many, remember, will be foreigners for whom the *Princess Anne* is their first taste of our great Queendom, and among the rest may be some of those ungrateful ratbags who go around enquiring why they fork out good money for a royal family, and I beg leave to suggest that, as far as opinion-formers go, your tautonym could just possibly be falling a trifle short.

I make no comment about the external state. Not being a household word where marine engineers foregather, I have no idea whether hovercraft are supposed to look scruffy. This may be a design-statement aimed at conveying an impression of workmanlike priorities, it may be saying "we are not a quinquireme of bloody Ninevah, our business is butting through the Channel in the mad March days, you get filthy out there, a burnish'd throne wouldn't last five minutes", but I cannot see why it should also be rusty inside. Nor why your gracious carpets should be so threadbare, your ceiling so egregiously stained, your plastic wall-cladding coming away, nor why, when I sat down in the seat you had so graciously provided, I should have made contact with its metal frame, due to its padding having been compressed by long use into one big lump at the side. I know why the seat-pocket in front of me sagged, though: it had empty whisky miniatures in it.

I sat in the smoking section. I had not been the first. When I opened the gracious ashtray, it was already stuffed, not with wrinkled butts alone, but with old sweet-papers, a wizened apple-core and an Elastoplast which had clearly done sterling service. Having winkled these out into a sick-bag remarkable for its pristine condition, I then went into the lavatory to wash, a task made simpler by the fact that your gracious tap was already running, and continued to run after I left, because it could not be turned off.

This did not account for all the moisture on the floor, however. Since we had been going for only five minutes and I had seen no-one else entering the lavatory, this had to have been the detritus of earlier voyagers, and I could not but wonder, ma'am, whether swabbing had gone out with the lash. And, indeed, whether both might not be brought back, were you to be graciously pleased to have a word with someone?

It is probably unseemly to mention your lid, but it may well be that the moisture on the floor was not entirely unconnected with the fact that your gracious lid did not stay up, a shortcoming particularly noticeable at 50 knots, especially as one has only one pair of hands.

Please forgive me, ma'am, for burdening you with all this, but I was concerned only with your good name. Be assured that had the scow been called *Sir Les Patterson*, I should never have given it a second thought.

SEPTEMBER

A Word in Your Eye

This could well be the worst week for hacks that there has ever been. This could be the week when our trade grinds slowly to a halt. By next week, pedestrians may be unable to negotiate the nation's pavements for the hacks in cardboard boxes panhandling small change.

Should this happen, it will of course be the result of that invariably retrograde force, progress; because we now inhabit an era in which non-necessity is the mother of invention, and those terrible words "technological breakthrough" indicate only that something has been subseded by something else. Since you ask, I do not know if the word *subsede* exists, but I do not intend to find out, because if I wanted to find out, I would have to drive to a shop which sells batteries so that I could put them in my magnifying glass, and if I did that I should almost certainly cop a parking ticket, and when you are faced by life in a cardboard box, you cannot chuck money away on little luxuries like that.

I cannot look up *subsede* without an illuminating magnifying glass, because my new Oxford English Dictionary is the micrographic version with about a million words per page, none

53

of which can be read without the Oxford English Magnifying Glass that came with it. What you do is, you put the book on the carpet, drop to your hands and knees, flick on the light in the magnifying glass, and slowly go blind and mad. I did not have to do this with my old OED, because it came in 12 volumes and eye-size print, but when it grew out of date through not having very important words like *yuppy* and *gazump* in it, I decided to buy the single-volume technological breakthrough that subseded it.

The effect was to slow down my work by a factor of n, where n represents the need to look a word up and then drive around searching for a meter within walking distance of a battery shop, before driving home and dropping to your hands and knees to go blind and mad. The cost in terms of words not written is, to take a rough figure, incalculable.

And incalculability stands poised for a quantum leap. This week, a lush brochure arrived from OUP announcing that the entire OED is now available on one floppy disk for only £480. Since you again ask, I do not know why it is *disk* not *disc*, I have been meaning to look this up for some time, and as soon as I get a couple of batteries I may, provided I have not replaced the OEMG with the new OEFD. If I do that, mind, I shall have to have bought a second computer, for if I have to keep removing the disk on which I am writing from my one computer in order to insert the disk containing the word I want to look up, it will take six months to write anything and I shall be in the cardboard box even sooner than if I had bought a second computer.

Why, though, should even two computers herald a cardboard box? Because they will slow me down yet faster than the OEMG they have subseded, thanks to a further technological break-through. A brochure speaks: ". . . now not merely a dictionary, but the most comprehensive thesaurus in the world. Hard-pressed for a synonym for *pier*? How about *causeway, cob, cutwater, dike, head, jetty, levee* or *mole*? All these and more can be found by searching for the word *pier* across the entire breadth of the dictionary."

Dear God, the very last thing a working hack needs is the most comprehensive thesaurus in the world! Especially when he has already subseded his typewriter with a computer: in the old days, he would type *To be or not to be, that is the question*, and, faced with the mucky option of Tipp-Ex, leave it at that and go on to the next bit. A word-processor, however, because it has a correctional facility (interesting that this term should also have subseded "prison") allows him, indeed encourages him, to think for a while and then write *To be or not to be, that is the problem*. And, after a further while, *To be or not to be that is the dilemma*. Which is how a hack's income gets cut in half. Now add to this a disk which, with 8 synonyms for *pier*, might well contain 50 for *question*. You could spend three years on a limerick.

Have I, then, decided against a second computer? Certainly not. It could be extremely useful, if it comes in a nice big cardboard box.

Eight Legs Bad

You probably think you know about godfathers. Oh yes, you say, godfathers, the people who make you an offer you can't refuse, ha ha. It has never occurred to you that the concrete might be on the other foot. You have not spared a thought for the godfather who makes an offer which is not only refused, but volleyed back with a counter-suggestion which he himself cannot refuse; because if you are a godfather, refusal is not an option. An example? Try this. A godfather is addressing his godson, whose 14th birthday it is the eve of:

"Would you like a cricket bat?"

"I'd rather have a spider."

"Is that some kind of electronic game?"

"No, it's a spider."

Do not ask about the dreams I had that night. Even though they weren't that bad. I didn't know they weren't that bad, mind, until the next day, when I fetched up against the reality. The reality was as bad as anything ever gets. If you think Winston Smith had a rough time in Room 101, try Regent Pet Stores. I thought they'd be all right when I found them in the phone book, because the phone book described them simply as imptrs of livestk, but one lk at the livestk they imprt, and yr hd swms. A rd mst clds the eys. Strng mn fnt.

"I want to buy a spider for my godson," I heard a far voice croak.

"Certainly," said the assistant. "We have a wide range of tarantulas, right up to the big bird-eaters."

He indicated these in the showcase below. You would not want to be a bird. These were not spiders you stepped on. These were spiders who stepped on you. They looked like crabs in toupees.

"He tells me," I said, squeaking hardly at all, "that he'd like a Mexican red-knee."

"Wouldn't we all?" said the assistant, a touch less accurately than he knew. "A lovely spider, the red-knee, but you try getting them. They are the flavour of the month."

I felt my mouth purse to a dot. You'll understand.

"What I'd suggest," he went on, "is a Chilean rose tarantula. Ideal. Only £35, quite docile, a very nice spider." He pointed to a glass box. There was a ball of khaki hair in it, the size of a fist. Very nice. Then it moved. Even nicer. Who can say why I stepped back? Doubtless, some silly atavistic twitch. I may have had a Chilean ancestor who made the stupid mistake of going out one night without his blunderbuss.

"When you say docile," I said, "do you mean friendly?"

"No, I mean quiet. Not aggressive. It wouldn't have a go at you unless you really upset it."

"What would upset it?"

"Clumsy handling. Particularly letting it walk all over you, and then startling it with a sudden move. A lot of people make that mistake."

I glanced past him, into Camden Town. There were a lot of people out there who let tarantulas walk all over them. We may have met, joked, shared a bottle. Will I ever know all there is to know about the world?

". . . holding them up to your face."

"Sorry, what?"

"I said the other risk is holding them up to your face. They have uricating barbs which they can project into your skin. Could damage your eyes. How old's the boy?"

"Fourteen."

"Would he know how to care for it?"

"I'm told he's got a giant millipede."

"Very different. They do not get mould, millipedes. If a tarantula gets mould, you have to know how to wipe if off. Still, he should be all right with a Chilean rose. Its bite is no worse than a bee-sting."

"Oh, good," I said. When I was young, boys wanted newts, mice, slow-worms, puppies. They watched *Lassie Come Home*. I do not know about arachnoid loyalty, but I would lay long odds that nobody is going to make *Chilean Rose Come Home*.

"I'll take it," I said. He reached below. "BUT HE'LL COLLECT IT!"

Only a few customers looked round. A parrot squawked.

I paid cash. I would have given a cheque, but the bank might have queried the writing. Unsteady? Of course not! Just a bit spidery.

Eight Legs Worse

The other evening, I found myself looking at what appeared to be a tiny broken bagpipe. It was leaking. It was, furthermore, leaking something black, and, furthermost, lying in what it was leaking. None of this would have mattered much had I found myself looking at it in, say, a gutter or hospital pedal-bin. I should merely have shuddered and walked on, but what I found myself looking at it in was a dish. The dish was on a table in front of me, flanked by knives, forks, and spoons; in short, all the accoutrements required if what you were going to do with a tiny broken bagpipe was not shudder and walk on, but eat it. Not that there was any if about it. I was a guest. The tiny bagpipe had been cooked by my hostess.

All the other guests had one, too, and they were uniformly thrilled by them.

"Oh, wow," they cried, "squid!"

"*Stuffed* squid," they elaborated, "oh, wow!"

"In its own ink!"

"Oh, wow!"

I looked at mine. I gave it a little prod with my fork. Ink ran out of it. Though not a household name where marine biologists foregather, I know why the squid has ink in it. It is so that it can squirt it out to put off predators attempting to eat it.

It works.

Not, mind, that it seemed to bother the others. They could not wait to tuck in. They sliced off the tentacles, they sectioned the body, they spooned up the ink, to choral yumming and oohing punctuated by brief autobiographical solos about how they'd always wanted to cook squid, it looked so *wonderfully* marbled, but they'd never dared, were they alive when you bought them, how did you kill them, how did you clean them, how did you stuff them, how did you find out how to . . .

My points exactly, as a matter of fact; though not, with me, uttered ecstatically, just brooded on internally. As, indeed, they had been with the first course, *shorba*, when everyone had shrilled, oh wow, isn't this that fantastic Yemeni marrowbone soup, yes it is, oh what's it called . . .

But I had managed to get that down all right. I had succeeded in persuading myself that wherever the marrow had been extruded, it was unlikely to have been from camel bones. I didn't think you could buy camel bones in Barnes. I would have heard. There were little fibrous lumps floating about in it, mind, that could have been goat, possibly hare (I looked up the recipe when I got home), but I managed to corral them under my reversed spoon, and I don't think anyone noticed.

Now, do not misinterpret all this gustatory whingeing: I am no culinary philistine, I have tied on the bib at many an ethnic bistro and not shrunk from having a cockshy at the arcane, even when I have not had the slightest idea what *yukyuk* or *bugatti* were and the patron lacked the bilingualism to convey. I have probably eaten wild toad in a wart sauce and held up my plate for more. I may even have been asked on the drive home whether I liked the stuffed nostril and not stopped the car to throw up. It is not a question of squeamishness over this exotic dish or that, only one of suspicion and unease when faced with the ambitions of the amateur. For while it is one thing to order tiger stew from an Ulan Bator restaurateur with three rosettes in the Mongolian Michelin, it is quite another to have it ladled out before you in Stoke Newington by an English ophthalmologist whose hobby is deciphering oriental cookbooks.

And there is a lot of that about, these days. The British – released from esculent restraint by both the Elizabeth David watershed and the immigration of countless entrepreneurs carrying woks, pasta-makers, clay ovens, *bains marie*, fondue sets, spice-mills, and all the rest, and bent under sacks of enigmatic herbs, vats of curious oils and liquors and yoghurts, and unfathomable lengths of dried animal – have become the acolytes of a hundred different cuisines, eager not merely to patronise the myriad professional establishments but, God help us, to emulate them to the best of their domestic ability.

A best which is not always good enough. While I applaud the ambition to cobble a *yasaino nimono* or a *cocida madrileño*, I have to say that admiration has too often wilted at the first forkful to leave me with anything but doubt concerning the frenzied competitiveness which currently holds the middle-class dinner-party circuit in thrall. I used to motor forth of a Saturday night thinking, good-oh, she's bound to kick off with that terrific salmon mousse of hers, hit us with a roast saddle of lamb to follow, and bring up the rear with a bread-and-butter pudding that would have Anton Mosimann putting the Sabatier to the wrist, but I do not think that any longer; these days I think, oh hell, she was talking abut Uzbek cooking when we met at that dinner party where I had to spit the bits of birds' nest into my napkin, I bet she's going to give us stuffed head of something after the larch-leaf purée, and he never stops going on about being something of a fromoisseur, ha-ha-ha, he's probably found this amazing dog's cheese which you have to wash down with emulsified arak, I shall no doubt be on my back in Bart's tomorrow with a "nothing by mouth" placard gummed to my drip.

It isn't just the cooking, either; it is the trust one is required to have in what went on before they got to the cooking, which is why, when that other evening someone asked how you cleaned a squid, I had a long pull of the Meursault and tried to think about something else. God knows what there is inside a squid. I remembered once watching *poulpeurs* preparing to market their catch on the Marseilles waterfront: they killed the squid by sticking their thumbs in the beaks and turning the bodies inside out, whereupon they chucked the entrails back in the sea, because there were poison sacs inside. Had my Barnes hostess known enough to do that?

I wasn't sure. So I just ate the tentacles. "Phew," I said, when the plates camé to be collected and an eyebrow raised itself over my little legless bagpipe, "That was one big squid! Do you know, I couldn't manage another bite."

Making Old Bones

In my younger days, I used to wonder what my skeleton looked like. I can even pinpoint the spark which detonated this speculation: I was studying *Hamlet* at the time, or at least hitting Gerald Finch over the head with it, because he sat in front of me for O-level English, and Mr Hoskins, to whom Lady Luck had dealt Finch and me from the bottom of her deck, enquired why I had struck my colleague with a cornerstone of our culture, and rather than bring up a girl's name, for these were gallant days, I replied that we had been having an argument about the play. Oh really, he said, because he had not been born yesterday, what kind of argument, and I said I wanted to know how Hamlet knew the skull was Yorick's, all skulls look the same, and Finch said the clown told him, sir, and I said why would Hamlet believe a clown if he told me how much water got poured into the average trouser, but would you believe anything a clown said to you in a cemetery sir, and Mr Hoskins said not necessarily, and that is an interesting point, Coren, well, fairly interesting, I shall try to find out whether skulls look different from one another, Mrs Gibson might know, her brother was in the RAMC.

He never got back to me, and it was *Guy Mannering* the week after that, but the question of what skulls looked like remained inside mine for some years. Nor only skulls, but the entire osseous sub-frame: it bothered me that I should never see mine, except in X-rays, where it always appeared hilarious: there were all these little grey bones, apparently not joined together, one serious sneeze and your entire infrastructure would fall to the bottom of your legs, leaving you to spread across the floor like a deflating blimp. I don't know why skeletons should be funny, perhaps it is nature's way of palliating *timor mortis*; a few years ago I fell off a horse and the osteopath I went to see had a skeleton dangling from his ceiling, pretty comical in itself, but when he hit it with a stick to indicate which vertebra I had damaged it started dancing, I laughed till it hurt, i.e.

immediately, and the poor quack said to my wife, is he always like this or could it be concussion?

He said it because she's a doctor, which brings me to last week's issue of the *British Medical Journal*, a comic she regularly passes on to me in the forlorn hope of bridging the marital gap, but for once it contained an article worth the unequal struggle. Entitled "A prospective study of alcohol consumption and bone mineral density", by Troy Holbrook and Elizabeth Barrett-Connor of the University of California, it concluded that heavy drinkers had stronger skeletons than teetotallers. Even better, while drinking strengthened bones, exercise weakened them; i.e. provided you eschewed jogging in favour of slumping in front of *Cheers* with a large Scotch, you could advance happily into old age knowing you contained a skeleton on which Eiffel himself could not have improved.

Not surprisingly, this lifted the spirits no end (oh, please, today's is a scientific treatise, if you want puns come back next Wednesday), especially since I could not remember the last time my lifestyle had received anything but an admonitory caning from the medical establishment: it is normally impossible for me to open a paper without reading that everything I do is lopping years off my life, unless I start fell-walking and eating a daily stone of bran I shall not see Christmas, so you may imagine my joy at learning that tipsy inertia was good for you.

And my wretchedness at subsequently discovering that it was not. For Troy and Elizabeth, canny as any hack, had saved the twist for the tail; arriving at their closing paragrahs and poised for statistical evidence that these strong bones of ours were proof against geriatric breakage, I found all hope summarily dashed. Can you guess why? Of course. "Studies of fractures and alcohol consumption are confounded by other risk factors, including increased likelihood of impaired vision and falling."

Alas, poor Yorrick! A' may have pour'd a flagon of Rhenish on your head once, he always liked a drop, he had bones like pike-staffs, but a fat lot of good they did him the night he walked right off the Elsinore battlements. Thought he saw a ghost, they say.

For Fear of Little Men

Disturbing, the people you suddenly find yourself having something in common with. Apart from anything else, it can ruin your syntax. Who would have guessed, when I awoke this morning, that within twenty minutes I should have become all but blood brother to Mr Hilton Cubitt, squire of Ridling Thorpe Manor, Norfolk?

If you do not instantly recall the name, permit me to remind you that he was a tall, ruddy, clean-shaven gentleman whose clear eyes and florid cheeks told of a life led far from the fogs of Baker Street. Got him now? Yes, indeed, the cove who turned up at 221b cried: "Well, Mr Holmes, what do you make of these?" and tossed a drawing on the cluttered desk which encouraged Watson not only to entitle this particular caper *The Dancing Men*, but also to reproduce the sketch itself, a Lowryesque number depicting a chorus line of high-kicking matchsticks. These, when Holmes had made of them what we had rather fancied he might, were revealed to be a code concerning an eternal triangle in which Hilton Cubitt, the squire on the hypotenuse, ended up drilled through the heart, leaving the other two sides faring hardly better, his rival Abe Slaney banged up for good in the Norwich slammer for doing the drilling, and the hapless Mrs Cubitt condemned to a life of filling the parish poor with soup.

How different, how very different, you murmur, from the home life of our own dear Cricklewood squire! Oh, really? What I murmur is where, when I need it, is a "trifling monograph upon the subject in which I analyse one hundred and sixty separate ciphers?" Try to locate this and you will soon find it is no use grabbing the Yellow Pages and saying, "Hello, sorry, it's J.R. Hartley again, you haven't by any chance got that monograph by S. Holmes on . . .?"

I went down this morning to collect the post, because I had heard the gate squeak, but when the post did not come through the letter-box, I opened the door, to find Jag the postman gazing at the gate's brick pier. Seeing me, he beckoned and I joined him, so that both of us could stare at the rough chalk drawing of a little man with, beneath it, three lines of flowing non-European text. Jag, who is Kashmiri, said: "Very odd, I think this writing is Demala." I asked him what Demala was, and when he said it was the language of the Tamils, I asked him what the words meant, and he said he didn't speak it, he just recognised it, which I suppose comes with being a postman, but he said the man who ran the Atlanta supermarket was Singhalese, and he would know.

I said I didn't think it was worth troubling him, it was probably just some passing kid, but Jag pointed out that the little man had an axe in his head, and if you saw it in Kashmir, it would frighten the life out of you, because it meant a death-threat.

Jag moved on, and I paused for thought. You did not want a Tamil contract out against you, I had heard about the Tigers, they did not muck about. I wondered if I might have inadvertently got on the wrong side of one, a meter-maid, a shop assistant, you never know, so I carefully copied down the drawing and the squiggles and I drove to Atlanta, and the owner asked who'd said it was Demala, and I said Jag, and he said Demala his eye, it was some kind of Arabic, look at these newspapers we stock and I did, and it was very similar, and I thought: have I sworn at any PLO meter-maids in the past few days, have I had a barney with any Hezbollah shop-assistants? Then Mrs Atlanta came out from behind the till and said that in Sri Lanka the axe-in-head routine wasn't a death-threat, it was just a curse, and I said fine, but what is it in Baghdad, and she shrugged and went back behind the till.

The Hampstead desk-sergeant said it looked to him like trampsign, he'd done a stint in Suffolk where tramps drew stuff on gates to tip the wink to colleagues about hot food, rottweilers, compliant chatelaines and so forth, and I said what do they mean when they stick an axe in a little man's head, and he said he'd never learned to read it, you didn't need it in the Met, and I said what's my best course of action, and he said why not wash it off the wall, so I did. I couldn't help thinking, mind, that the passing of Sherlock Holmes had left a bit of a gap.

On a Wing and a Prayer

I am standing, this morning, in the front garden of Number 6, Basing Hill, a street but half a mile from my own, and I am hurtling down the arches of the years. I am heading for December 14, 1920.

It is noon, that Tuesday, and 6 Basing Hill looks good. Why should it not? It has only just been built, a fat redbrick villa, a signal of post-war recovery, a home fit for a hero. And, in a few minutes' time, it will have one; though not before it has stopped looking pretty good. It will be looking pretty bad, by then.

But before we meet him, we must drop in on a more literal yesterday, to find me standing in line at Cricklewood Timber, and behind me an elderly gent; who, as we waited, said: "When I was a kid, this was an airport. It was the first international airport in England."

I looked at him. You can never tell with elderly gents.

"Cricklewood Airport?" I said. "When was that?"

"1920," he said. "It had its own customs shed. You could fly to Paris and back for 18 guineas. Also Brussels, some days."

"Next!" said Cricklewood Timber, and I paid for my wood, and I drove home, and I thought, what the hell, they can only ask me to pull the other one. So I telephoned the RAF Museum at Hendon.

But they did not snigger. They said, yes indeed, Cricklewood Airport, come over, we have books, magazines, records, and within the hour I was walking past a sculpted mural which ran *"Flight without feathers is not easy." Plautus, 250–184 BC*, and into both the library and a tale which Plautus himself might have quilled in evidence.

It started joyously, mind, fit to lift the heart of one who has never sought, as you know only too well, to find any twinkle beneath this village's thick bushel. For in 1912, I discovered, Handley Page set up an aircraft factory off Cricklewood Lane. It had a good war, and so flourished that, in September 1919, HP Transport was formed, initiating a scheduled service to Paris and Brussels, flying a modified HP 0/400 heavy bomber carrying two crew and six passengers.

My heart pounded! *Cricklewood* an international byword, even in Flemish! Not, mind, that my predecessors were grateful: a cutting from *Aeroplane Monthly* read: "Locals have complained of soot being driven down their chimneys by passing HPT aeroplanes. They also consider it unsafe to stand on the top decks of tramcars." What ingrates! For me, the blood sang, the cheeks glowed. Here, at last, was local history!

They did not glow for long; moments later, they had drained. For history has its ups and downs, notably aviation history, and you will guess the rest: we have been there before, you and I, we have learned that when it comes to Cricklewood, it does not stay. This time, it was *Flight* magazine for December 16, 1920, which turned Cricklewood's claim to fame into its claim to notoriety: "On December 14, a few minutes after noon, G-EAMA struck a tree during take-off from Cricklewood, and stalled into Number 6, Basing Hill. The pilot, mechanic, and two passengers were killed. Four other passengers were slightly hurt."

And that, I'm afraid, is the Cricklewood milestone which the world will remember: look, as I have now looked, in *The Shell Book of Firsts*, but do not look under Airline Glory, look under Airline Disaster. Mere weeks later, they stopped the service, they took our customs shed away, and they looked on Croydon and found it good.

Yet it is not grief alone which brings me musing, this morning, to the garden of 6 Basing Hill. I promised you a hero, and you shall have one. So let me end with words more splendid than any I could cobble, from C.H. Barnes's account in his *Handley Page Aircraft since 1907*: "Eric Studd, the sole occupant of the nose cockpit, was thrown clear, but when the rescue party arrived he was nowhere to be found, and was feared lost in the wreckage. Next day, however, he was seen in Paris, having no clear memory of how he got there; apparently, he had been knocked out in the crash, and on recovering consciousness in the garden had remembered only that he had to go urgently to Paris, so he had taken the Underground to Victoria Station and travelled thence on the Boat Train via Dover and Calais."

OCTOBER

Ourselves to Know

Just how dangerous a little learning is, I have just learned. Earlier today, I received a letter from Elisabeth Bolshaw, editorial director of Hodder & Stoughton, saying that their "Teach Yourself" series, launched 54 years ago, is to be relaunched next April, and that the accompanying fanfaronade would be incomplete without the plaudits of people willing to attribute their present success to their past study of this inestimable self-help library. If I was one such, particularly if I still had the volume on my shelf, would I complete and return to her the following sentence: "*I consider my greatest achievement to be . . .*"?

This letter has deeply unsettled me. Not because I am offended at Elisabeth's inference that my life's work gives off an autodidactic niff suggesting I picked up the trick of it at Foyle's for half a crown, but because it so happens that I do have a Teach Yourself book here. I did not remember this, though, until she reminded me, and when her letter jogged me into seeking it out was when my deep unsettlement began. It is unlikely that it will ever end.

71

The seeking-out took place in the attic, because the volume was not on my shelf, it was in a small box containing the books my father left behind when, in 1988, he embarked upon that journey on which none of us needs to take along something to read. The box was small because my father wasn't a reader: his library consisted mainly of old AA books and such tosh as Reader's Digest felt would improve when shrunk to a tenth of its size and given away to those who cared as little about good books as about good magazines. Thus, when my old man died, it wasn't need but sentiment that required me to hang on to his books, and as attics are for sentiment not need, that is why they are there.

And why, a couple of hours ago, I was, because Elisabeth had made me recall not only the familiar blue-and-yellow cover of another book my father owned, but also that I had never even glanced at it to see what it was he had wanted to teach himself. I opened the box.

He had wanted to teach himself Danish.

I opened the book. A date was pencilled on an endpaper.

He had wanted to teach himself Danish in 1958.

I closed the book for a bit. In 1958, my old man had wanted to teach himself Danish. He was 46. I was living away from home, so I did not know he wanted to teach himself Danish. I knew it now, but I did not know why he wanted to. Nor did I know whether my mother knew that he wanted to teach himself Danish, or if she did, whether she knew why, either. Since she, too, is now dead, everything about my father's teaching himself Danish is unknowable.

But is it unguessable? I opened the book again. Several words and phrases were underlined in red. They did not represent a continuum: my father had dipped and selected. He had, for example, ignored Exercise 9, *Den Grimme Aelling*, altogether. He did not want to know about ugly ducklings. But he wanted to know about Mols. Mols is where Molbos live. Exercise 26 retails how the Molbos chase storks, the point being, as far as I could work it out, that the Molbos are dimwits. Why would my old man want to know that? And why would he have underlined, elsewhere, such words as *smuk* and *ulykkelig* and *cykel* and *det gor mig*, why was he storing the ability to say "beautiful", and "unhappy" and "bicycle", and that he was sorry? How could this bizarre lexical jigsaw best be assembled? Had my old man, unbeknown to his family, sneaked off to Denmark, fallen in love with a dim but beautiful Molbo, made her unhappy, felt the need to apologise? Or was he apologising because he had knocked a male Molbo off his beautiful bike while the poor dope was out chasing storks? Or maybe my old man never went to Denmark at all, maybe he had only a mid-life dream of going, of cycling to Mols, finding a beautiful airhead, telling her he was unhappy, apologising for his ignorance of ducklings . . .

I shall never know. I have been able to teach myself nothing of my father. I do, though, now know the Danish for "king". It is "kong". This means that when *King Kong* is shown there, it is billed as *Kong King*. Not perhaps my greatest achievement, Elisabeth, but something.

Uneasy Lies the Head

While I have always brandished scepticism in the face of such jolly legends as the one which has it that wee Jimmy Watt saw his mam's kettle rattling and immediately began working out how to get it to pull the 8.14 from Leeds to Euston, I nevertheless accept that many a scientific discovery is born of happy accident. Until Wednesday, however, I had never been able to test this personally: despite my having spent 19,764 days wandering the planet, each of them had gone by without my fortuitously stumbling against something which, after I had tinkered with it a bit, would leave that planet a better place.

But on Wednesday, the search for a housewarming present led me to a Notting Hill junkique where, having judged the options of a clockwork parrot that shrieked "Guten Morgen!" and a vase which let you shove flowers where Gladstone's brains ought to be, I plumped for a Great Exhibition glass paperweight the size of a tennis-ball, containing Queen Victoria, Prince Albert and a couple of dogs; who, having set off for a stroll on a fine clear morning, could have their day ruined by anyone who cared to shake their premises, covering its inhabitants with snow. Set on a yellowed ivory base, it was patently worth every penny to anyone born yesterday, so I forked out and drove it home.

It was only after I had unwrapped it that I noticed that the newspaper it had been swaddled in was slightly moist. I ran a finger over the paperweight and found that this was slightly moist too. That it had suffered a minor leak, possibly as the result of rolling around in my glove compartment, was obvious as soon as I allowed the whirling storm to settle: everything was covered in snow, except the Consort's stovepipe hat, which was above the level of the fluid. The tableau had thus taken on a far more sombre cast than hitherto, suggesting that the luckless royals had been cheerfully walking their dogs on, say, some frozen pond, when the ice had suddenly given way beneath them.

Since you could not warm a house with so brokendown a gift, I turned the paperweight this way and that, finally working out, from the continued seepage, that the fluid was emerging between the glass ball and the ivory base, since when I tightened this latter the leaking stopped. Obviously, all that was required was for me to unscrew it completely, refill the ball with water, and screw it up again.

After a minute or so I had an unscrewed base, an empty crystal ball, an unpronounceable hemisphere of green glass grass with one royal and one dog attached to it, a little pile of white flakes, and, separately, another royal and another dog. Quite why Queen Victoria and one of her dogs should have detached themselves from the green glass grass I did not know, nor why Queen Victoria, when I picked her up to try to find out, left her little head between my thumb and forefinger. Upon closer examination, however, I discovered that all these discrete components had originally been held in place by tiny pegs, so it was with great relief that I carefully reassembled the whole, put everything back in the ball, filled it with water, and screwed the base on again, very tightly.

It was perfect. Until that is, I shook it. When I did that, the snow eddied up, which it was supposed to do, but so did Queen Victoria's head, which wasn't. After a bit, Her Majesty's head came down again, but, as it did so, it passed her dog, going up. Since I do not understand, you may be surprised to hear, hydrodynamics, I cannot tell you why, when I shook it again, Prince Albert now shot upwards through the falling snow, thankfully missing his wife's head coming down, but colliding with her descending dog. It was horrible! It was hilarious! What did I have? I had an animated Chagall.

But I also had, unquestionably, an invention. By happy accident, I had produced an original artefact, and now that I have also detached Prince Albert's head and the other dog, I have a 3-D narrative kaleidoscope of infinite themes. Each time I shake it, a different tale of grand guignol appears. It is nothing less than a tiny Victorian telly.

Catch me giving this away! I intend to stay here playing with it until they come round to put my blue plaque up.

Hair Today, Gone Tomorrow

I suddenly find myself in a position to knock over sub-post-offices with impunity. Should that pall, I might alleviate the subsequent boredom by slipping into a seedy hotel with, let us say, an unemployed Iberian soubrette, confident that neither she nor the chatelaine would be able to identify me and cozen a few bob out of the tabloids. And were I to find myself in the *Question Time* audience, I should, when Peter Sisson's finger beckoned, be able to spring to my feet, curse the assembled parliamentary ratbags in language so simultaneously foul and libellous that the BBC switchboards would fuse to molten solder, and then vanish into the night without any risk whatever of recrimination or writ.

For in all these cases, they would be looking for a man with a heavy moustache. It would have been the first thing they had noticed, and the only thing they remembered. That is the kind of moustache it is.

You are right to pause and glance at the cover photograph. But you are not right to mutter, oh, grown a moustache, has he, is that all, stuck for a subject again, you can always tell when a columnist is going off, up comes a moustache. Think, and you will quickly realise that merely growing a moustache would not allow me the full range of subversive fun of which the examples listed above are but the waxed tip. I would have to keep shaving it off and instantly growing it again, wouldn't I?

I have not grown a moustache at all. I have bought one. In fact, I have bought three: I should not want the sub-postmistress or the chatelaine to leap from their chairs in the middle of *Question Time* shrieking: "That's the man!", so I have bought an M2, an M4 and a C102, although those unhabituated to mooching about in Tavistock Street will need to think of them as a Groucho Marx, a Jimmy Edwards, and a Che Guevara. I look knockout in all of them. Children flinch; dogs run, yelping.

None of this would have come about did the London parking system not make work for idle hands. A couple of days ago, due for lunch in Covent Garden at one, I arrived at 12.30 to give myself time to find a meter, but struck lucky immediately. It was bang opposite the premises of Charles H. Fox Ltd, purveyors of make-up to the theatrical trade since 1878. With time to kill, I walked across. It was a great window: hung with racks of moustaches and beards and side-burns. It enabled me, by variously crouching and sliding, to position my reflected face so that I became a hirsute spectre. At which point, a thought appeared on the horizon, no bigger than a man's goatee. I looked at my watch. I went in.

When I came out, I was walking behind a dark brown M2. I also had an M4 and a C102 in my pocket. A snip, as it were, at £7.40 each, and – if you look like Groucho, puns come easy – not to be sneezed at; not, at least, for those uncertain of the properties of spirit gum. When I arrived at Boulestin, my host, who was watching the door from his table and has known me for 20 years, did not recognise me. I took off my hat and stared at him. He looked away. It was only then that it dawned on me that I should not be able to come clean – thanks, Groucho – but would have to wear the thing right through lunch, because however great a fool I might look with it on, it would be nothing to the fool I would look if I suddenly whipped it off. So when my host said: "How long have you had a moustache?" I just smiled, and since the crinkling lip didn't nudge it off, I needed to say nothing.

But I have never had such trouble with a menu: I had to find stuff you could poke through a fringe with impunity, punity being detritus adhering to an M2, which might itself end up adhering to a napkin. I chose cold sauceless prawns, grilled sole, and cheese, none of which I fancied, and I let trapped winedrops trickle down for collection on my chin. Thank God I didn't buy a beard. £18.50, since you ask.

I got away with it, though. It stayed on, and it has been on and off a fair bit since, although M4 and C102 have remained pristine in their packets. You need to work up to a Jimmy or a Che. Just one thing nags at me: pristine has two senses, and when I look at the labels, the words "100% human hair. Made in Hong Kong" gives me pause. Is someone, I wonder, even now sitting down at a table in Seoul's fashionable Crispy Airedale Inn, opposite a host saying: "How long haven't you had a moustache?"

Anything for a Laugh

Today is a big day for both of us. What you are in for today is a work of scholarship. It is a particularly big day for me, for it is exactly 30 years since my last work of scholarship: in May 1962, in the middle of my PhD course at Yale, I was driving back to New Haven when it was suddenly borne in upon me that I was not in the middle of my PhD course at all, I was at the end of it. I had had enough; I drew from my pocket the sponge I had been keeping for just such an emergency, and threw it in. Though it meant that I should not now be able to impress an accident mob by crying "Let me through, I'm a doctor!", loosening the victim's clothing and explaining to him that Crabbe was not the last of the Augustans but the first of the Romantics, it seemed a price worth paying.

However, while you can take the boy out of academe, you cannot take academe out of the boy. There will always be the twitch upon the thread, even after 30 summers, and, this morning, no sooner had I slit open the post than the dawn came up like thunder, I could 'ear the footnotes chunkin', and the siren cry of "Come you back, you British scholar!" rang out irresistibly across the steep Atlantic stream.

For the letter was from the State University of Kentucky, home of blue grass and orange chicken, and signed by Steven H.

Gale, Endowed Professor of Humanities. Just how endowed he might be, not to say just how human, you may well soon find yourself pondering, but for now it is enough for you to know that he is seeking "solid scholars" to contribute to a book he is editing for Garland Publishing. What Garland Publishing is I cannot say, but if it is concerned with things to hang round the neck, Millstone Publishing might have been a wiser choice, given not simply that the professor's book is called *The Encyclopaedia of British Humorists*, but also that the humorists for whom scholars are still being sought are William Godwin, E.M. Forster, George Saintsbury, the Smith Brothers, Robert Southey, E.J. Trelawney, and Windham Louis. For though all are unquestionably major comics, it takes a Kentucky sense of humour to spot it, and it will, furthermore, take a singularly solid scholar to interpret this to a wider audience.

Happily, cometh the hour, cometh the man.

If I may quickly clear up one or two uncertainties, Windham Louis is of course not to be confused (an easy mistake for the unsolid) with either Percy Wyndham Lewis, the hilarious Vorticist, or D.B. Wyndham Lewis, the Catholic biographer who sometimes traded under the name of Timothy Shy. Windham Louis played baritone kazoo with the Mound City Jug Blowers (fl. 1929) until his lip suddenly went in the middle of "Coal Cart Blues". Though uproarious at the time, this might seem scant basis for a humorous reputation, until we compare it with the career of the Smith Brothers. My researches have unearthed that these were not even entertainers (unlike, say, George and Weedon Gross, who will I'm sure be well known to Professor Gale), they were but jobbing builders whose doors always stuck. Not funny at all, until the solid scholar points out their imperishable legacy to English farce.

We are on surer ground with Robert Southey, who, though often described as Wordsworth's straight man, nevertheless made Dorothy laugh, just the once. It meant, of course, the end of Bob's sexual ambitions, but mention it in Kentucky, 200 years on, and folk become hysterical, drawing comparisons with Saintsbury's *History of English Prosody* and even Trelawney's account of the death of Shelley, made the funnier by the fact that Trelawney was actually present at Leghorn when the fish-nibbled remnants of his friend were finally gaffed.

While some solid scholars remain uncertain if Shelley's father-in-law William Godwin also saw the comical side of this, it seems very likely, given the fun-feast of his *Enquiry Concerning Political Justice*, which I have heard Kentucky barmen recite till the tears ran. Whether, mind, this could be matched by the rib-cracking Marabar Caves routine from *A Passage to India*, I cannot judge, having merely read it.

And as E.M. Forster always said, it's the way I tell 'em.

NOVEMBER

Not Much to Bragg About

If, like me, you were one of the 12 million watching *A Time To Dance* last Sunday, you are probably still a bit bothered about it this Wednesday. For, towards the climax, or one of them, of Melvyn Bragg's rollicking chronicle of fell swoops, you saw something.

It wasn't very much, and it wasn't there for very long, and any of you who sneezed, or even perhaps laughed, may not have seen it at all, but for those of us who take our membership of the Lord's Night Observation Society seriously, it was of a significance out of all proportion to its ostensibility. And I choose that last word with more than usual care, for these are delicate matters, so delicate indeed that non-Latinists will have, I'm afraid, to ask close and trusted friends to fill them in on the precise etymology of my choice.

As to the observed item itself, let that same delicacy refer us to the dainty lexicon of the antiques trade and simply call it the property of a gentleman; appropriate enough in this case, since the gentleman himself is not only knocking on a bit, he is also what Sotheby's catalogue would describe as of heightened colour and somewhat distressed.

He is Mr Ronald Pickup, playing a 54-year-old bank manager, and the story so far is that he has become, one is tempted to say willy-nilly, passionately enmeshed with Miss Dervla Kirwan, playing an 18-year-old set of attributes likely to bring hurly-burly to the deep peace of the Sabbath night, and John Selwyn Gummer hardly back from Evensong. Probably still unzipping his anorak.

For they are tricky things, anorak-fastenings; many of us who sport them have learnt, when contemplating a hike, to set aside a fair proportion of the day for getting in and out of our rainwear, and it is thus but one of the myriad remarkable features of *A Time to Dance* that Pickup and Kirwan are able to divest themselves so rapidly not only of these complex items but also of the stout boots, thick socks, heavy sweaters, long-sleeved shirts, thermal underwear, scarves, mittens, woolly hats, and all the rest of the cumbrous paraphernalia required for going up Magnus Pyke, or whatever it's called.

They can do this, of course, because love laughs at locksmiths, so that, with an alacrity evoking the great days of Mack Sennett, they are quickly in a position to hurl themselves upon one another and begin running up Mary Whitehouse's phone-bill.

Which activity, as you know, presupposes a certain state of readiness on Ronald's part, if there are not to be tears after bedtime. Hardly a problem, you would think, given that Dervla is the best thing to have happened to him in a month of Sundays, a fortnight's anyway, and that, from the internal evidence, a good time appears to be being had by all.

But let us look at the external evidence. We could not, as I mentioned at the outset, look at it long, but it was long enough to register that Ronald was in no shape to do what the script, never mind his eager paramour, required of him.

"Hallo," I said.

"Is there anything to which you would wish to draw my attention?" said my wife.

84

"To the curious incident of the dog in the night-time," I replied.

"The dog did nothing in the night-time," she said.

"That was the curious incident," I remarked.

The exchange did not go quite like that, of course, it was somewhat shorter, but what my wife and I say to one another in the privacy of our own hilarity is nobody's business but ours.

Now, ever since the curious incident, I have been thinking about it, long and hard; and it has become curiouser and curiouser. What was this scene for? For verisimilitude: the play concerns the irrepressibility of passion, and we must, apparently, see them at it. But if what we see is them apparently at it, ie not at it at all, whence the verisimilitude? They might as well have shut the bedroom door on us, offered a few convincing grunts, and left it at that.

I am afraid that, like Ron and Dervla, I have come to no firm conclusion in this affair. All I know is what *Ecclesiastes* tells me, just after it has told me that there is a time to dance; which is that there is a time to embrace, and a time to refrain from embracing.

Balloon Game

You could say it was none of my business. It was not in my tree, it was in the council's tree, outside my house and my jurisdiction, and it was therefore the council's business. But what I say is *civis Barnetus sum*, which translates roughly as "left to Barnet council, it will be there for six months, or until some kid chucks a brick at it and the brick goes through somebody's window, viz mine".

Apart from which, it looked horrible. This being the time of year it is, it is bad enough beholding bare ruin'd choirs where late the sweet birds sang, without having to behold something quite as ruinous to a bare choir as this. Shakespeare didn't know how lucky he was: true, there may have been chips and dog-ends littering the feet of Elizabethan trees, but at least Raleigh did not bring rubber home from the New World. When Shakespeare looked out of his bedroom window, he did not find an enormous red balloon looking back at him.

Looking, moreover, with two blob eyes and a crescent grin: you know the face I mean, the circular minimalist one created in the Sixties so that lapels and tee-shirts could proclaim the virtues of substances which gave you two blob eyes and a crescent grin. Since I did not want this in the tree outside my bedroom window, I ran downstairs, screwed a couple of drain-rods together, and went outside for a bit of a poke. It was a tough balloon. It did not go bang. The grin grew grotesquely twisted, but the cheeks held, until, with one bound, the face was free and floating, very slowly, down.

The end of the problem? The beginning.

I had, until that moment, assumed that the face had broken away from some home-toddling infant for whom a tube of Smarties, a wedge of birthday cake, and a balloon-string had proved too much for one small mitten, but it was not so. This was an adult balloon. Moreover, and despite its vacuous grin, it was a serious one. I could tell this, because it was Belgian, and you do not get much more serious than that. And I could tell it was Belgian because it sported a label that had been attached to it by one Martin Verlaan, who had done the attaching at a carefully printed-out address in Liège, which, I'm embarrassed to admit, gave me immoderate pleasure, because this meant it was a Walloon balloon.

However, even such agreeable gift-horses have to have their mouths examined, which was where the problem I mentioned began. For I had Martin's address, but what was I going to do with it? He had dispatched the balloon in the hope that someone finding it would write back to him, and common courtesy, common market courtesy indeed, seemed to require me to let him know that the thing had successfully negotiated the 250 miles which separate Liège from Cricklewood. Furthermore, that's only if you're a crow: if you're a balloon, frail prey to every breeze and thermal, you could have been anywhere, you could have got to my tree via Kyoto and Bogota; so, Martin apart, did I not owe the balloon itself, after all its hard work, something more than a pin and a wastebasket? Wouldn't it want Martin to be proud of it?

And yet, and yet. Who is Martin? What kind of man sits in a room in Liège with an oxygen cylinder and a bag of balloons, filling the international welkin with his name and address? And wanting, moreover, mine in return, because that's what the label invited, in half a dozen languages. He might be merely an amateur meteorologist, he might be merely unemployed, he might be merely lonely, but he might, too, be raving mad. You can never tell with people who float balloons out of Belgian windows. Would I want to enter into a correspondence with a crackpot? I wouldn't even want to enter into a correspondence with an amateur meteorologist. I should have to find out what an isobar is in Flemish, and since I do not know what an isobar is in English, I cannot see much future in further contact, you know how it is with pen-pals, one thing leads to another, and before you know it there is an anorak standing on your mat holding two fir-cones and a rain-gauge and asking to stay the night so he can pass on his occluded front anecdotes.

I think my best course would be to put the balloon back in the tree and let Barnet deal with him. That's what council tax is for.

Just Grate

A riveting *Inspector Morse* on Wednesday, I thought. Four different fireplaces. One massive job in white Carrara marble with offset slips and a double-corbelled support; a jolly little knotted pine number with oval paterae and a burnished semi-inset cowl; an elegant mahogany example of the Adam style, carved swags and husks, fluted jambs, and, as you would expect, inner mouldings of trefoil and dart; and the fourth a simple yet charming granite arch with just a gunmetal dog grate and what I am certain was a Welsh slate forecourse, although my wife remains unbudgeable from the conviction that this was in fact York stone. A woman impervious to informed screaming, I'm afraid.

You're not going to believe the next bit. Astonishingly, the mahogany item was *almost identical* to the mantelpiece against which Stephen Fry was leaning at the delightful party I went to last Sunday morning at Claire Rayner's Harrow premises! How about that, eh? True, I swear. Sadly, though, the house had so many fireplaces I had to give up making rough sketches after a bit. You'll understand. The head begins to swim. And sadder even than that was the fact that although Stephen is the most engaging conversationalist I know, and one I run into all too rarely, I was unable to concentrate on a word he was saying because of what he was leaning on. Nor did it help that he is a large cove, and fidgety. Kept throwing his arms about and obscuring bits of moulding.

Worse was to come. By one of those extraordinary coincidences with which mantelwatching is rife, when Stephen opened up again that night in BBC2's *Common Pursuit* I was unable to pay any attention to what he was saying this time, either. Or, indeed, to what anyone else was, for the play not only had several serious fireplaces in it, it had one so utterly *right* that I had to go and lie down. That night, I hardly slept.

Monday wasn't too bad. I worked all day, thereby running into no fireplaces at all, and we didn't watch the box that night, we went to see Steve Ross at Pizza on the Park, which doesn't have fireplaces, so I could listen to Steve's stunning act, and I was doing fine until the interval, when I fancied a cigar but they didn't have one, so I went next door to the new Lanesborough Hotel, and that was it. They've put a fireplace in the foyer you wouldn't believe. By the time I'd finished examining it and got back, Steve was half way through his second set. My wife said: "Where's the cigar?" and I said: "What cigar?"

I've suddenly realised you may not know what this is all about. I may just have neglected to tell you that since February 5 I have had the men in. Certainly, you do not know that the men have reached the point where they need to put the fireplace in. They want me to choose one. They have been wanting me to choose one for a fortnight. I have read all the fireplace books there are. I have been to all the fireplace shops there are, and I tell you it is not easy going into places called Grate Expectations and Feeling Grate and Burning Sensations and Old Flames, but you have to.

After that you start looking at every fireplace in every house you go to, and when that is not enough to bring you to a decision you start looking at every fireplace in every house you do not go to, i.e. in films, on television, at the theatre, but no ballet, unless of course it's *Nutcracker*.

And does all this help you come to a decision? I'll tell you what all this helps you come to. Do you remember when the great Bobby Fischer gave up competitive chess? He said he knew it was time when he found it impossible to walk up Park Avenue without seeing chess moves in all the paving squares. What happened to him after that, or where they might have put him, I do not know, but I may be in a position to tell you any day now. If they do put me in the same place as Bobby, we may very well play a game or two. I cannot claim to be a grandmaster, but if he gives me one of those little horses and a couple of towers, he shall find himself with a run for his money.

Provided I can concentrate. If Bobby's room has a fireplace, I may well have problems.

Living on the Edge

In the far-off time, Best Beloved, when men not only beat their plough-shares into swords, but came round to your premises to saw your railings off and cart them away on the grounds that they intended to beat them into Spitfires, there was something of a shortage of metal. It was not, fortunately, so short that anyone actually tried to make Spitfires from the railings which were collected, because a cast-iron Spitfire would not have been much of a match for an Me109, and we should all have ended up (if you can manage for a moment to suspend your disbelief) in a Europe dominated by Germany, but it was short enough to mean that you couldn't buy new pots, pans or cutlery.

Thus if, when carrying your wartime dinner from stove to plate, you noticed that the pan which had set off with a Spam fritter in it had arrived without it, and if, when you looked through the hole in the pan, you further noticed that the cat was licking the last of the Spam from the lino, you knew that you would have to run out into the street and look for a man on a tricycle. Or, since we are now coming down to cases, your mother would have to run out into the street, because you were only five years old and No. 32 had caught a packet the night before so that there was glass everywhere, and Mr Churchill couldn't risk five-year-old boys getting hurt, you never knew how long the war would last; a caring PM could not chance future cannon fodder being excused military service on the grounds that it had copped a Blighty one in 1944 by falling down and cutting itself outside No. 32.

Your mother would have had no difficulty at all in finding a man on a tricycle. There were a lot of them about, in those days. They wore khaki balaclava helmets and mittens with the fingers cut off, and Great War medals on their old herringbone overcoats to show that they were not conshies, they had done their bit, they had gone right through the Last Lot, but the most interesting thing about them, if you were a five-year-old boy, was that their tricycles were the wrong way round. Yours had one wheel at the front and two at the back, whereas theirs had two at the front and one at the back. This was to give stability to a fourth wheel which was set above the front two, a big stone wheel, this time, cleverly activated by a gear that simultaneously disengaged the other three wheels to enable the man to pedal it round and sharpen knives on it.

And on the back of his tricycle he had a wooden box with pan-menders in it. These were pairs of discs, in a wide variety of sizes, centrally secured by a little bolt so that, placed either side of the hole in a pan, the discs could be tightened together to form a fritterproof seal. Which meant that, after a bit, your mother came inside again with her recycled pan, kicked the cat, and, since that had been the last of the Spam, rooted around in the larder to see if she had any fritterable corned beef.

Usually, though, you ended up with a pilchard. Meanwhile, the house would be penetrated by a noise immeasurably worse than any air-raid siren, because the pan-repairer would have wheedled her into having her knives ground; to this day, I cannot pass a Tesco pilchard display without my teeth being set on edge.

Now, since we have at last arrived at this day, let me also come to my point. Not three hours ago, but 50 years on, I heard that sound again.

I had of course, interim, heard sounds a little like it – when getting a key cut, say, or inadvertently bumping into Janet Street-Porter – but never the exact sound, not only louder and shriller and nastier than any seeming-similar, but also, as in the austere lang syne, rattling the casements of a suburban street and setting a hundred dogs off. I do not have the space to detail here the myriad resonances it triggered, but if you imagine Marcel Proust not biting into his biscuit but instead having a man on a tricycle put a sharp edge on it, you will not go far wrong. I smelt Welsh Nutsmoke, I tasted cod liver oil, I heard Vera Lynn banging on about the White Cliffs of Dover, I felt my bare knees chap. And, my mother no longer being in a position either to do it or to stop me from doing it, I ran outside.

There was a man on a tricycle. A single wheel at the back, two at the front, and a big stone one above them. Parked at the kerb opposite, he was sharpening a kitchen knife. He did not, however, wear a balaclava helmet or fingerless mittens or a herring-bone overcoat, nor sport a row of Gallipoli ribbons. He was not even old. Early twenties, probably.

Twenty-three, as it turned out. I'm allowed to cross the road, these days. I also discovered that he had a good second from the University of Warwick, in politics and economics, and that he had had it since the summer of 1991. He had had precious little else, mind; a few bar jobs, some shelf-stacking, a spell in Santa's Grotto going ho-ho-ho, fairly hollowly at a guess. And then he had got on his bike. He had spotted it in a warehouse he was helping to demolish when he was on the lump, he had cleaned it up a bit, and now he was in the itinerant knife-grinding business. Also, yes, he could repair pots and pans if required, he didn't carry potmenders, he didn't even know about potmenders, they probably don't do them now, he said, all this Teflon et cetera, but a lot of people wanted duff utensils renovated, new handles put on, dents banged out, you'd be surprised, these days.

No, I wouldn't. Nothing surprises me, these days. What it does do to me need not detain us, but were Mr Malcolm Rifkind to turn up at my front door with his handcart and a requisition order for my railings because, since nobody else now wanted to build the Eurofighter, Britain had decided to go it alone, that wouldn't surprise me, either.

Gone With the Wind

I should not be writing this at all. I should be writing a battle anthem. I should be sitting here in my grey breeches and riding boots and my grey jacket with the yellow frogging and epaulettes and my plumed hat, and quickly dashing off something for my men to march behind. Downstairs, my crinolined wife would be snuffling decorously into a lace hankie, while the daily (since I unfortunately lack a trusty black manservant) would be honing my sabre, oiling my Navy colt, and getting my horse out of the garage.

And don't say I'm too old. When Robert E. Lee was given command of the Confederate forces, he was exactly my age. For rebel generals, 54 is the prime.

Mind you, I say dashing off, but it would not be an easy anthem to write. Since it was Winston Churchill who maintained that there was no more stirring a battle march than *Dixie*, I should be happy enough with the tune, but chiselling new lyrics to fit it is an altogether trickier matter: if you would care to pause at this point and attempt to sing "Look away, look away, look away, South Cricklewood!" you will immediately hear the snag. It is that intrusive third syllable. Were I putative commander of the forces of all Cricklewood, of course, it would be a doddle; but it is the word South that is the problem.

In, I fear, every sense. For I have just returned from France to find that we are two Cricklewoods, now: amid the pile of post jamming the front door was a letter from the Borough of Barnet addressed to me in somewhere called South Cricklewood, and when I instantly rang to enquire about this hitherto undesignated territory, I was told that henceforth, for administrative purposes, Cricklewood would be divided into North and South, the border being Cricklewood Lane.

Border? I cried, *border*?

I know that I need not elaborate my horror. I have wearied you often enough over the past few years with my bid to register Cricklewood upon the national consciousness, to give to airy nothing a local habitation and a name, and now here was Barnet stomping in, with inky blots and rotten parchment bonds, to cleave that nascent identity in two.

But then I thought, hang on: might those drear words "for administrative purposes" be no more than nervous bureauspeak to deflect me from a far grislier truth? Might something quite horrible have happened during my absent month? Might the blame lie not with Barnet at all, but with Gorbachev? For since we know, now, that the noise we heard in November 1989 was not that of a wall being dismantled but of a wall being cannibalised in order that a hundred other walls could be erected in a hundred other places, could it be that dear old Cricklewood had, while I was briefly gone, supped upon that ghastly cocktail of fissiparousness and exclusion which has left all Europe reeling and brawling?

I ran up here to the loft, and looked out. All seemed quiet enough. No obvious Balkanisation going on, no shots, no shrieks, no pockmarked masonry, and from what I could see of the *soi-disant* border half a mile away, the buses seemed to be trundling back and forth along it without any undue interference from mines. But do you know, even as I looked, it was suddenly borne in upon me that there were indeed two distinct Cricklewoods, bisected by the Lane: the noisy bustling industrial North of dark satanic home improvement centres and mighty used car lots, and the indolent bucolic South of tweezered lawns and Hoovered patios, where, though space forbids cotillion and point-to-point, the tinkling laughter of lovely women and the sage opinions of authoritative men nevertheless punctuate the scented gloaming as the Chardonnay goes down and the flakes of half-eaten vol-au-vent pirouette in the tastefully floodlit breeze; and since such cultural disparities have ever been a precursor of bitter clash, could Barnet be trying to tell me our time is nigh?

I feel a chill wind rattling the casement. Any day now, the Northern forces may pour across the new border under some such pretext as, say, freeing our au pairs, and life as we know it, gracious, gentle, elegant, will disappear forever.

Though not, if I can just sort this anthem out, without a fight.

Antique Hay

D o you recall the pivotal moment of *The Muppet Movie?* Kermit, having hopped three thousand miles to Holly-wood in pursuit of his dream, contrives an audience with Tinseltown's leading mogul, brilliantly played by a length of horn-rimmed felt.

"What do you want?" the mogul asks the frog.

"I want to be rich and famous," replies Kermit.

The mogul jabs his intercom. "Bring me the Rich-And-Famous contract!" he barks.

You would certainly have recalled it last Thursday morning, had you been standing with me in the nervous throng milling atop the wind-blown summit of a north London hill. We were, mind, not the highest point on that hill, because above us rose the neatest possible symbol for what we were all doing there: an antique television mast, formerly the property of a favourite auntie, in nice condition considering its age, some restoration evident, but still a splendid example of its period. Had we given any thought to what it might be worth? Good God, no, this had never crossed our minds, we had always cherished it for itself alone, it had great sentimental value, it was like one of the family ...

We were at Alexandra Palace because the BBC was at Alexandra Palace. Not, now, to transmit beyond it, but to film within it, for it was here that *The Antiques Roadshow* had put up its caravan, just for one day; which was why thousands of old carrierbags had convened thither from all over the metropolis, in hope not merely of becoming rich beyond the dreams of avarice, which I had expected, but of realising dreams beyond even that, which I had not.

At first glance, however, you wouldn't have guessed they wanted wealth and fame. You would have guessed they wanted sanctuary. The Great Hall looked like an Oxfam transit-camp, filled with long glum lines of refugees from who knew what catastrophe; they clutched their pitiful bundles, they pushed

95

prams containing not only wailing children, but busted clocks, dented samovars, mildewed pouffes, chipped vases, wizened moose-heads (such heartbreaking detritus, you would have assumed, as they had been able to snatch up as flood or rebel tribesmen bore down upon them), and in their hands they held the precious tickets which, presented to the officials at the dozen desks towards which they shuffled, would entitle them to a bowl of soup and a blanket.

It was only as you mingled that the truth emerged.

"I could very well get on camera with this," said a man beside me.

"What is it?" I said.

"A mechanical-dog stick." He drew it from his hold-all. It was a walking-cane with a spaniel's head. The man pressed a button, and the dog's mouth opened and its tongue popped out. "They're always on the lookout for novelties," he said.

"Is it valuable?" I said.

"Shouldn't think so," he said. "That's not the point."

"Right," said a man in the parallel queue, firmly. "Take this teapot. Remind you of anybody?"

I hesitated. "George Robey," said the man. "They'll lap it up."

A small boy ran back to his queueing mother.

"I've got Hugh Scully's autograph," he said, waving his book.

"You stay with me," said his mother, "you'll get David Batty's. You'll prob'ly be on television as well. I've brought Grandad's weasels."

She had them under her arm. They were in a glass dome, frozen in the dismemberment of a gull. She caught my glance.

"Very photogenic," she said, "am I right?"

"Are you sure this is the correct queue?" I said. "Batty's ceramics."

"He'll like these," she said. "Anyway, Eve wants to take a picture of me talking to him."

Eve nodded; the Polaroid bobbed on her chest. This family were true collectors. They collected stars. For that, with 14 million viewers a week, was what the *Roadshow's* experts had become. Which was also why the punters lugged their old junk around the country; not because it could be valuable, but because it could make them stars, too. For while few might find something in the attic to make them rich forever, many might find something to make them famous for 15 minutes.

Thanks for the What?

Something has really got up my, er, has really set my teeth on, nose, up my nose, this morning. Not to put too fine a thing on it, it could well be the straw that broke the, the, oh God, big animal, like a horse but lumpier, does that ring a, think of that man from was it Arabia, they made a film about him, anyway he rode around on one as I recall, he blew up a train in somewhere or other during one of the world wars, you must have seen it, it had the one in it with the moustache, swarthy bloke, bridge-player if my memory serves me right, unless it was snooker. You know who I mean.

Where was I? Oh, right, I wanted to tell you about this infuriating item I read in the *Daily*, the *Sunday*, hang on, I cut it out and put it down somewhere, I was reading it in the kitchen, no, the dining-room, the kitchen was where I went to get the scissors to cut it out with, so I probably carried it back into the dining-room, if you'll just bear with me I'll go and, ah, no, it's all coming back, I put it in my jacket pocket, but it doesn't seem to be, wait a sec, I wasn't wearing a jacket then, I didn't put my jacket on until well after, or rather just before, anyhow there was a ring at the back door, front door, and I had to go out and, hold on, it was my dressing-gown pocket, I read it while I was making the, or did my wife make it, anyhow I'll just nip upstairs and . . .

Sorry I've been so long, I was standing in the bedroom staring at my dressing-gown and then I had to go back downstairs and come up again to try to remember why I had gone upstairs for my dressing-gown in the first place, and then after I went back upstairs it suddenly occurred to me that I hadn't telephoned someone I had to ask about something or other, Mr, Mr, could be Geoff, my wife knows who he is, but she's gone out to see her, as you were, down to the, oh God, tall redbrick building on the corner of, you must know the road, it's named after a king, not an English king, a king of, a king of, the country had something to do with ointment, I get this picture of a tin, anyway it'll come to me in a bit, and then I can phone her there and ask her about this Geoff person, or possibly Brian, she may know what I did with his number, too, I know I wrote it down in the back of, I tell a lie, on the cover of, anyway I was in the middle of reading it when he phoned the first time, thick yellow paperback with some kind of a crustacean on, could have been a crayfish, it didn't have claws, yes it did, he won the Booker Prize a year or so back, might have been 1987 now I think about it, if that was the year we went to Bimini, or was it the Whitbread? I think I may have met him once, we were at this hotel, sorry, party. Airport. Not Gatwick.

Anyway, I've got the dressing-gown now, so that's all right, I'll tell you an interesting thing about this dressing-gown, it wasn't always blue, it used to be, um, it used to be a different colour, wait, wait, we never actually went to Bimini at all, we *planned* to go there, but at the last minute there was either an air-controllers' strike or one of the children caught could it have been measles, no, now I think about it they had measles while I still had the Volvo.

God knows why I wanted to dye the dressing-gown, I must have had slippers it clashed with, in which case why didn't I dye the slippers instead, hold on, it was mumps they caught when I had the Volvo, I remember driving them down in the middle of the night to see old Dr, young Dr, and now I think about it it wasn't Bimini we didn't go to, it was Rimini.

Well I never, here's where my cigarettes and lighter are, in my dressing-gown pocket! Well, that's it then. End of story.

God knows what this is in the other pocket, it appears to be a cutting from *The Sunday Express*, I wonder how on earth that got there, it says Glaxo are spending £100 million developing a drug called ondonsetron designed to cure absentmindedness in the middle-aged, have you ever heard anything so preposterous, one *hundred* million pounds at a time like this, it is not as if it was even a problem, we all know absentmindedness is just a figment of the, what's the word, this is not to be borne, it is all quite scandalous, I may very well write a piece about it.

The Last Days of Pompeii

Yesterday found me in a brothel. It knew where to look. It knew that an ace reporter did not let the grass grow; if the nation was undergoing yet another of those prurient convulsions periodically detonated by a great man's moral hiccup, then it was the bounden duty of everyone with a trenchcoat and a bit of shorthand to raise the double standard high and march towards the sound of the sniggering.

You know me, though: a tireless seeker after truth, I eschew the easy routes. I am not a man to lurk behind the Kellogg's display in some Balearic Tesco, idly waiting for a fugitive pillar of society to push his trolley past, nor am I, when the editorial cry goes out to round up the usual psychiatrists, content simply to cobble their clichés into another lecturette about why men blessed with radiant and fragrant domesticity should occasionally find themselves doom'd for a certain term to walk the night. I dig deep. If necessary, I am prepared to go back two thousand years.

Or 1914 years, to be precise, which is what we can be in this case. We know the exact hour at which, on August 24, 79 AD, time stood still for lovers, and never started again. We can walk into the little whorehouse behind Abbondanza Street and know that one moment the occupants of its five snug cubicles were at it like knives, and the next a ghastly miasma had whistled through the tiny window and gassed them where they frolicked. For the earth had moved for them: the top had blown off Vesuvius, and that was that: after a bit, a blanket of pumice dust tucked them in for a couple of millennia, until it was time for caring archaeologists to get their brooms out, because tourists had begun queueing at the gates, waving currency.

Which was where I was yesterday, shot thither by an inaugural Euro Express Daybreak, which leaves Heathrow at breakfast, gets you to Pompeii only 1914 years earlier, and has you back in London for dinner. Plenty of time to learn all there is to know about life in 1st-century Italy, and more than enough if you are an ace reporter intent only upon discovering what it was like to be a Latin lover when they were actually doing it in Latin. Indeed, one of the many ancillary delights of pottering about a Pompeiian funhouse, for those of us once forced to grapple inadequately with Hillard and Botting, is to imagine those old stucco walls echoing to the din of joyful gerunds and ecstatic ablatives shrieked by people able to do it totally spontaneously in the course of doing something else, without having to stop and wonder whether all their adjectives agreed with all their nouns.

Any doubt about what it was they were doing is soon dispelled by a glance at the old stucco itself. The miraculously preserved frescoes are both a menu and a testament to what can be achieved if you are blessed with roomier premises than a Vauxhall parked, briefly, behind King's Cross station. As for kerb-crawling, it was so sanctioned by the civic fathers that phalluses were chiselled into the paving-stones to indicate the optimum route to crawl, and so graphically that, twenty centuries on, a party of Japanese visitors plodding soberly up Abbondanza Street in front of me suddenly fragmented like a flock of startled pigeons, giggling helplessly and allowing me to nip past into Number VII before the rush. And what a poignant spot it was: five tiny rooms, each with a little stone bed and a little stone pillow, each sporting its fresco depicting the imaginative shenanigans of the ancient lusty, forever panting and forever young, embracing not merely one another but strangers 2,000 years younger, in the world's oldest continuum.

As we ace reporters say, it made you think. If you were not careful, you could easily find yourself nibbling at the old chestnut about state-run brothels, and before you knew it, you might have had to face the one about Pompeii's being dedicated to Venus and how much easier it might be to worship something a little more sympathetic than our own celibate divinities, and soon after that you might even have had to ask yourself how far we have crawled in 2,000 years.

I was too smart to do any of that. I made an excuse and left.

DECEMBER

Pasts and Presents

He is standing in the dimly-lit tunnel, his back turned, a yard ahead of me. I know that top hat, I know that green frock-coat, I know those buckled shoes. Forty-odd years have passed since last I saw him, but you don't forget stuff like that. I reach out to touch his shoulder; I hesitate; I withdraw the hand.

If I make him turn, what shall I see? He was 50, then; what is he now? Mrs Bates in the motel cellar, shrivelled to a wizened pippin? But I brace myself; I am a big boy. Softly, I call his name. He looks around, and faces me.

He is 20 years younger than I am. The blood congeals. Clearly, he has a painting in his attic. The Picture of Dorian Holly.

I was ten when I first saw Uncle Holly. Selfridge's had reindeered him in from Greenland to help out Santa, which was big news in the age of austerity: there were stores which had a job mustering one bran tub, let alone two. You had to go to Selfridge's, even if the last thing you wanted was to perch on an alien knee and tell a pack of lies about being a good boy on the off chance that the knee would then come up with a Daisy air pistol. You had to go, because your parents had waited a whole war to do parental things like that, so you went to Selfridge's tea room and a girl in black bombazine brought everyone waffles, and you ate the waffle and your mother spat on her hankie and wiped the waffle off your face because Santa didn't like sticky children – a long day could mean a beardful of jam – and then you went to queue outside Santa's Grotto, but you never got an air pistol; you got *Five Go Off To Smuggler's Top*. Hardly surprising, really, given that it was Enid Blyton who hit on the idea of getting Uncle Holly from Greenland. The woman knew a thing or two; you do not shift half a million books a year by sitting around waiting for the Booker Prize to get invented.

And that was the last time I saw him, because I grew up the next year and had a paper round, and by Christmas I could buy an air gun without having to tell anybody how good I'd been; but Uncle Holly carried on at the same old stand until 1980, when Selfridge's finally decided to whip round for an engraved bracket clock and a ticket home to Greenland, and that, one had assumed, was that.

One had assumed wrong. This week, Selfridge's defrosted him and brought him back, and I thought: why not trip down the arches of the years? The tunnel I found him in was, however, not his alone, nor even his and Santa's: they are mere sub-tenants of the Dinosaur Grotto, at the portal of which there is a large fur dinosaur in a nappy, labelled £499. Childhood has come a long way since the 1940s: never mind an air pistol, I know where you can buy a Kalashnikov for £499.

Nor, when you enter the grotto, do you see either Santa or his jolly oppo. You do not even see dinosaurs. You see three rubber chickens. You see them, furthermore, flying through the air, because they are being juggled by Mr Suitcase, and it is only after you have negotiated Mr Suitcase that you see your first dinosaur. It is a blue velour triceratops, and it is watching two tyrannosauruses in green dungarees doing something ambiguously rhythmic to one another, while around them all manner of typically Mesozoic activity is going on – dinosaurs surfing, dinosaurs hang-gliding, dinosaurs weightlifting, dinosaurs watching other dinosaurs on television, to the point at which the caring spectator begins to wonder about the future of little Damian.

Little Damian's mother is in front of me as we file through. "It's nice for him," she says. "He's doing a project on dinosaurs."

Oh good, I think, this will sort him out; palaeontology will henceforth hold few surprises for little Damian. I should rather like to be there when his teacher learns that iguanodons rode motorcycles, but I do not say anything because I have just, at last, spotted Uncle Holly along the tunnel, and have, as you have heard, my own anachronisms to suffer.

Good God, I am even older, I note, than Santa himself. How can I climb on his knee and tell him what a good boy I've been, and may I have a Ferrari and Michelle Pfeiffer?

Card Index

I have received a Christmas card from a dog.

When I first drew it from the envelope, I did not think it had been sent by a dog, I thought it had been sent by a human being who had bought a Christmas card with a dog on it. I did not think it was much of a card, mind, because the photograph of the dog was not much of a photograph. The head of the dog was all right, but the far end of the dog was a bit out of focus, and the house beyond the far end of the dog was not only even more out of focus, it was wonky as well. This was not a photograph at all, it was a snapshot.

None of which is to say that it mightn't have been a professional Christmas card. It is quite hard to tell, these days, with so many charities on the go; I have already received a fair few cards with ill-drawn blobs on the outside and, on the inside, information about dolphin shelters and acid rain and the like, and this canine item might very well have been one such. The dog looked relatively hale, but you never know, it could have had some psychiatric ailment, and as to the quality of the snapshot, perhaps it was the best that the Miserable Dog Trust or whatever could afford. It would be irresponsible to chuck good money away on Lord Snowdon if the Hon Sec had an Instamatic.

But when I opened the card, it just said: *Merry Christmas and a Happy New Year from Bruno* in type, with "... and his humans, too!" added in green ink. No signature, no address. I closed it and looked at the dog again. It was a total stranger. Nor could I identify the fuzzy house. It has a fuzzy car outside it, possibly a Volvo, but it's only a guess.

This kind of thing has been getting worse, over the years. When I was young, people sent one another cards with robins on. They were not in aid of Robin Relief, nor was the bird a family pet whose turn it was to do the cards that year. You opened them, and they said "Merry Christmas to you and yours from Jim and Millie Nugent, 'Erzanmine', Walnut Crescent, Uxbridge". You knew where you were with cards like that.

But then, instead of the robin, the personalised card came bob-bob-bobbing along. This had the senders on the front, generally two adults you recognised, surrounded by several infants and a cat. As a shorthand method of keeping abreast of events in households you never visited, it served, I suppose, its purpose. As Yules passed, you watched hair fall out, waists thicken, spectacles arrive, children lengthen, cats degenerate. Sometimes the family moved to the country, and a horse joined them. Sometimes they emigrated, and the Eiffel Tower or the Great Barrier Reef materialised behind them.

But, as Yeats used to scribble gloomily on his own cards, things fall apart, the centre cannot hold. A Christmas would come along when you noticed a new baby sitting by the car, and you thought, "Hallo, they're a bit old for another kid," and then you looked at the picture again, and it wasn't the same wife as last year. An extreme and deeply unsettling example of all this was the card we had a couple of years back from a man I didn't know at Oxford 30 years ago. He had married the ex-wife of a man I did know at Oxford, and, when she remarried, she was the one who carried on sending cards. These cards had her and her new husband on, plus a couple of new children standing next to her old ones. Then her second marriage broke up and her ex-husband married again, but hung on, apparently, to the old Christmas card list. We now get an annual card from two people we don't know standing next to a lot of big unfathomable children who could belong to almost anybody.

And now we have an unfathomable dog. Why the hell Bruno couldn't have had his surname or address printed, who can say? Might it be some kind of test? People with dogs, I find, expect you to recognise their pets, so it may well be that Bruno's humans have got him to sort out the wheat from the chaff. If they do not receive a card from me in return, my name will be mud.

I can think of only one solution to all this. I shall put a notice in the personal column of *The Times* to the effect that Mr Alan Coren wishes Bruno to know that he will not be sending any cards this year.

Brown Study

I wonder when I shall be able to go out again? I wonder when I shall stop looking radiant?

Some qualification is necessary here. An image, I know, has come into your head. Possibly of the Queen Mother. It will not help today's farrago. Radiant is not my description of how I look. Radioactive might be closer: that man, you might say, were I able to go out again and let people look at me, is pumping out roentgens like there is no tomorrow, which in his case there very possibly isn't. You would then cross the road sharpish. If you had children, you would gather them up and run.

For radiant is John Lewis's description of how I look. It describes a face which seems to have gone three rounds with Mike Tyson; indeed, a glance at my hands shows one of them apparently bruised enough to suggest that I even managed to get in the odd right jab before the lights went out.

But these brown blotches are not bruises at all. They are radiance. It said so on the sachet. This arrived last Saturday, in the envelope containing my monthly John Lewis statement, and it was gummed to a glossy leaflet with *Pour Vous* on it, beside a tasteful study of a blotchlessly radiant young woman inviting me to Discover The Secret of Sun-Free Tanning with something, called Esprit de Soleil, available exclusively at the Lancôme counter of John Lewis stores.

With Esprit de Soleil, the blotchless young woman continued, I could look radiant all year round. Most exciting of all, I could experience it now. All I had to do was apply the contents and wait three hours, remembering to wash my hands afterwards, because Esprit de Soleil contained oxybenzone.

I walked around for a bit, as anyone would who was not entirely certain whether he wanted his face oxybenzoned. After the bit had expired, I noticed that the sachet was in fact a double, so I detached one half and rubbed its contents on the back of my hand in a test run. After three hours, the back of my hand had gone rather impressively tanned. Radiant, even. Since I had as yet put nothing on my face, you would not have thought, looking at me, that I had been in a fight. You would have thought: "This man is a concert pianist. He practises all day in a room where the sunlight falls only on the treble end of his Steinway."

Thus encouraged, I opened the other sachet and began smearing it on to my face. It was only then that I realised I

110

might not be the *vous* it was *pour*, since, unlike the tumble-tressed girl on the leaflet, I have a face which extends to the back of my neck. I needed a radiant head, too. There was, in short, not enough stuff to go round; or, rather, go over. Indeed, even unbald men's heads must be bigger than women's, because I could manage no more than nose, forehead, one cheek and half a jaw before the sachet emptied. Never mind, I thought, being slightly radiant is better than not being radiant at all.

But I did not become slightly radiant. I became partially radiant.

It is Monday as I write, and I do not know what to do. You will say: "Run round to John Lewis and buy a whole bottle of the stuff", but I cannot do this. Even were I able to nerve myself to the assistant's muffled cackle at vanity's come-uppance, I doubt that I should be allowed to get as far as the Lancôme counter. For I have spent two solitarily confined days pondering this affair, and I have reached the conclusion that this would be to play into John Lewis's hands. Not because I think all this was a trick to get me to shell out real money on a big jug of oxybenzone, but because I think it was a trick to get me to shell out real money for something else. I do not believe I shall get as far as the Lancôme counter. I believe that, as I enter, I shall be instantly identified, and pounced upon by John Lewis heavies.

For the bill accompanying the free sachet drew my attention to the fact that my account was now two months overdue. Can it be that John Lewis sends sachets only to his serious debtors? Knowing the irresistible lure of buckshee radiance, has John cunningly trapped us all into a self-stigmatisation curable only by his exclusive antidote, an item not available until settlement of outstanding bills is effected?

Might, in short, this radiant blotch on my forehead be nothing less than the mark of Cain?

Angry Old Man

I have been in this business for a long time. That is how I know it is a business. I did not think it was a business when I went into it. But after I had been in it for 15 minutes, I had a rough idea and 32 subsequent years have served only to endorse that first impression. So when writers talk about being in the business, they are not fending off the risk of pretension, they are not coyly dissembling the conviction that it is an art, a vocation, a passion, they are merely stating the facts.

The 15 minutes began at 6.30 p.m. on September 17, 1960, at the publishing party for my first book. I had never been to a publishing party before, but, convinced that it would be swarming with poets, novelists, playwrights, and all manner of belletrists, I therefore saw to it that my corduroys were suitably wrinkled, my suede shoes scuffed, and my tie askew, and that the hair I conveniently then had was flopping in unkempt Bohemian hanks. I also selected the 29 bus against my trusty Rudge, because I knew that I should leave the party not only roaring drunk but with knuckles so barked from thumping other writers that I should be unable to grip the handlebars. What we should all have been thumping one another about were such topics as whether poets had become derelict of political duty, whether alienation was not a cul-de-sac into which the theatre had recklessly driven itself, and whether the novella was an unaccountably neglected form, and we should have chosen drunken thumping as the resolution of our differences because that's what writers did, look at Scott, look at Dylan, look at Ernest, look at Brendan, one minute you have a full bottle of Jack Daniels grasped by the base, next minute an empty one grasped by the neck.

Then I walked into Faber's little soirée. Everybody was wearing a charcoal-grey suit and discussing contractual sub-clauses, television adaptations, agents' percentages, fees on the lecture circuit, second serial rights in New Zealand, and second homes in the Perigord. The only time a voice was raised above a decorous murmur was when some luminary was moved to complain of cavalier treatment at this literary lunch or that when he had been forced to speak second after some major dietician or minor royal, at which observation everyone else, rather than sticking one on him, merely capped his anecdote.

I have, since then, been to perhaps a thousand similar gatherings, and they have all been the same. For all their brilliant eccentricity and perilous intemperance, our literary lions might have been ovenware salesmen or dental technicians convened to launch their autumn ranges.

Until last Sunday night. Last Sunday night, the Writers' Guild of Great Britain threw their annual awards dinner; they threw it at the Dorchester, they threw it in black tie and shimmering gown, and they threw it for and with those who do their business in great inkwells. There were, after a suitably corporatist dinner, ringing keynote speeches from literary industrialists, and then there was an awards ceremony in which senior literary employees and entrepreneurs received those mantelpiece gee-gaws which generally presage a smart career move.

And after four hours, John Osborne got up; more or less. He was there, as the evening's crescendo, to receive the Guild's lifetime achievement award. He made it to the podium, a fortunately sturdy item, where he began to ramble rudely, so that, very soon, a lot of tuxedos were urging him to get off, and a lot of other tuxedos were growing furious at the irreverence being directed towards a great, albeit legless, man. Eventually, Alan Bleasdale, Alan Plater and Alan Rickman helped him from the dais (I would have joined in had my wife not shrewdly pointed out that four Alans might invite more ridicule than was strictly called for), but not before skirmishes had broken out between the factions incensed by his unbusinesslike behaviour and those incensed by the lack of pity for a stricken hero. When I tell you that female independent television producers wept, you will have some measure of the moment.

But what nobody appeared to recognise was that this was exactly how a great writer *should* behave. I had waited 30 years to see a literary genius get drunk and trigger a chic assembly into war, and that it was done by Osborne, at the fire in whose belly we have all warmed our hands for so long, was quite the most joyous part of the entire business.

Money for Old Rope

Returning from France on Monday, I was astonished to see no mention made in any of our papers of the tercentenary of the death of Sir John Sash. My astonishment was the greater precisely because I *had* just returned from France; from, to be even more precise, the town of Saintes. And because, to be most precise of all, of a pain in the neck.

Since I see that the eyes of one or two of you are now rolling around in your head like marbles in a saucer, I have to conclude that you are either as ignorant or as forgetful as our national press; so, if the rest will bear with me, let me briefly rehearse Sash's remarkable story.

On the evening of December 14, 1686, Mad Jack Sash was playing whist in the Rapscallion Club with his inveterate companions the 2nd Earl of Sandwich, the 3rd Earl of Cardigan and Mr Henry Guinness. The game had been going on for two days, stopping for neither sleep nor victuals, the players sustaining themselves exclusively upon tobacco, in consequence of which the room had grown so thick with smoke that it was impossible to distinguish the suits; whereupon Sash declared his intention to open a window.

At this, Cardigan said they would all freeze to death, and that he was popping downstairs to find something to slip over his shirt. After he had gone, Sandwich and Guinness observed that as the game now lacked a fourth, it might be an opportune moment to seek something to eat; this they did, leaving Sash to open the window. It was only then that he discovered the casement to be unopenable; with its hinges and catch both rusted shut, the window left Sash no option but to hack off its fittings with a poker. Since he now found himself with an aperture too large for comfort, he ingeniously contrived, with the aid of two curtain cords and a pair of fire-irons, to hang the window back in place, leaving a small gap which could be increased simply by raising the window and allowing the fire-irons to act as counterbalances.

Not long after he had finished, Cardigan, Sandwich and Guinness returned, Cardigan wearing a horse-blanket in which he had sabred a ragged hole for his head, Sandwich bearing a salver of food, and little Guinness carrying a wooden firkin.

"How d'you propose to deal in that?" said Sash to Cardigan.

"It needs working on," agreed Cardigan, "and since I cannot get a hand out, would anyone care to feed me a tidbit from Sandwich's tray?"

Sash picked one up. "This appears to be two slices of ham with a piece of bread in between," he said, "as a result of which my fingers are now covered with mustard."

"It needs working on," admitted the 2nd Earl. "May I propose that we have a drink and cogitate, Guinness?"

After they had all spat into the fire, Guinness said: "It needs working on, of course. Apart from anything else, there's the smell. Shall I throw it out of the window?"

"You'll have to open it a touch," said Sash, whereupon Guinness pushed up the window and leaned out. He was still pouring when the window hurtled down again, severing his neck and allowing his head to roll, with remarkable etymological exactitude, down Pall Mall.

"It needs working on," said Cardigan, after a bit.

"Nonsense!" retorted Sash. "You have merely to be careful. Like my late cousin Charlie, Henry has stepped through a window into history."

And so it proved. While long years were to pass before the heirs of the other three were to achieve the requisite refinements,

Sash's masterpiece, notwithstanding his own sad decapitation 300 years ago last Monday, has remained unaltered. I can attest to this, because when we walked in on that day to relieve the house of its stuffiness, a window fell on my neck, as indeed so many of them so often do.

And Saintes? But two days earlier I had been gazing at a statue to its favourite son, Josef Guillotin, who, the plinth claimed, invented his eponymous gadget in 1790. That France makes no mention of Guillotin's plagiarism does not of course surprise me, but that England should ignore it I find intolerable. Sometimes I feel that when it comes to the treatment of aristocrats, there is little to choose between us.

JANUARY

And Did Those Feet?

W e didn't get corn circles in Cricklewood. You need corn. This left us marginalised from the great summer debate, and glum. For urban life is short on magic, and even mystery is brief: you usually conclude, after a bit, that it wasn't the fairies who nicked your milk, nor a warlock's curse that flattened your battery. Likewise, few midnight knocks betoken a time-warped Saracen or a basketful of royal foundlings; it is generally a minicabbie looking for Fulham.

What envy, then, we felt, down here, for lucky rural folk! We, too, wanted to squat in moonlit fields, craning to catch Titania treading a measure in the cereal, or listening out for a tinny voice to cry: "We mean you no harm, Earthlings, see we bring Venusian toffees, and humorous T-shirts for your emir!" Even a hoaxer would have left a welcome hiccup on the flat oscillograph of our lives: what fun to have sprung out on Jeremy Beadle, just as he finished rolling his bogus circumference, and thrashed him to within an inch of his life!

But it was not to be. The corn got cut, the winter came, the country people snuggled happily beneath their thatch to dream of next season's yet weirder phenomena, and, down here, we ground our jealous teeth and reconciled ourselves to puzzling out, instead, the mystery of the single currency. It may not have come from Pluto or Cloud-cuckoo-land, but it was as close as we were ever going to get.

Until this morning. This morning, I looked out from an upper window on to a lawn thick with hoar-frost. Pretty enough, but that was not what made the heart lurch: for there, etched into the twinkling rime, was a huge circle, so impeccable as to suggest a 10ft set of compasses. No tracks led to it, nor any away; though shortly, as you may imagine, mine did both. I was on the lawn in a trice.

They were the footprints of a gigantic hound! Was this the fabled corn circle of the Baskervilles? Alas no; I peered closer, freezing a knee: these could not belong to any dog. No dog has a heel and five toes. Then again, no human being has a foot two inches long. And then even more again, what beast, be it canine or human, can materialise in the middle of a large lawn, leaving no trace of its passage thither, impress a perfect circle, and vanish as trackless as it came?

I ran back into the house, and up to the attic. You know the kind of box: it always has *The Coral Island* in it, and *Kennedy's Shortbread Eating Primer*, a few dead bees, and right at the bottom, *Tracking Made Easy*, which some dumb uncle bought you 40 years ago because he thought you might need to identify spoor left in your parent's fifth-floor flat, could be an okapi, funny place, Cockfosters.

So I took it outside, and I knelt again, with the book open at British mammals, and you would not believe the variety of feet that walk upon England's mountains green, but when it came to what had walked upon Cricklewood's garden white, nothing. As far as Capt. John Wills-Bourne, late of the Selous Scouts, was concerned, this footprint did not exist.

So I telephoned the Natural History Museum.

"It is most probably," said the NHM woman, in that gentle but firm voice so often employed when talking to the deranged, "a hedgehog circle. This is how they feed."

"It is not a hedgehog's print," I said, "and even if it were, the hedgehog would be the size of a bulldog. Anyway, how could it leave no track but the circle?"

"It might," said the woman, "be a stoat or similar dropped by an owl. If it was hurt, it might have run in a circle until the owl retrieved it."

I consulted *Tracking Made Bloody Impossible* again, to be certain.

"It is not a stoat," I insisted, "nor similar. And whatever it is, an owl could not have picked it up. A condor possibly, but this is Cricklewood."

"If you fax us a photo," sighed the woman, "we'll try to identify it."

So I went upstairs for the camera, and the sun was now streaming through the landing window; which I thought no more about, until I was back on the lawn. The frost had gone. The circle with it.

Theories c/o *The Times* on a postcard please. And country folk need not apply. They've had their turn.

Laughter in the Dark

A night or so ago, I was slumped in front of a sitcom containing no sit and even less com (to pedants protesting there can be no such thing as negative comedy, I will say only that they were not there), when something suddenly jolted me from my torpor and hurriedly mustered a number of brain cells which, up until then, had understandably believed themselves to be having an evening off.

It was a single girlish peal; which, while it may well be the sort of item you would regularly run across in a Barbara Cartland paragraph, you would not normally hear issuing from the audience of a television comedy. And hardly had it died than it was followed by a solo baritone guffaw, which you would not normally expect to hear, either. For this audience was, like so many, a canned one, opened long after the programme had been finished and spooned out to interlard the script with responses the director felt were required if viewers were not to think they had stumbled across some little miasma tossed off by Strindberg in one of his glummer moments.

Now, canned laughter is usually nothing more than pre-recorded gales of ensemble cackling, which suddenly burst on the ear from nowhere and then as suddenly stop, much as if one were passing a madhouse as someone briefly opened a door and shut it again. The laughter is not differentiated into hoot, titter, and chortle; it is a wodge of noise chopped from the soundtrack of some genuinely responsive audience and grafted on where needed. It is a laughter transplant.

This laughter, however, was fascinatingly different. Though it had been added afterwards, it had also been individuated to suit each joke, misunderstanding, walk-into-door, and so on. It occurred to me that for the first time in my experience, I was being instructed not merely when to laugh, but how to. This is merely an aside, the sound track was saying, requiring only a chuckle, so do not waste a howl on it because there is a really big boffola treble-take coming along any minute now, when we shall be asking you to pull all the stops out.

One of the best things about really bad television is how much wool you can gather while staring at it. I thus began to speculate on the manufacture of this new laughter: since it had clearly been assembled from countless different bits, were there laughter-banks, perhaps, where donors – selected for their inordinately high laughter count – were handed a joke and shown to a cubicle in which they did their private thing? Did they shuffle out again, somewhat sheepishly, and hand their cassette in at the desk, so that it could be matched to a register of directors with sterile scripts? Were they paid for this? Was it controlled, to safeguard the world against one day filling up with unwanted by-blows, i.e. bursts of hysterical giggles turning up uninvited in the middle of, say, *A Time to Dance*?

I could not answer this, not simply on its own account but also because it had started umpteen hares, now thumping their hind-legs on the carpet with more than mere unseasonal madness; for why should responses not turn up in other programmes, if they were the appropriate responses? Indeed, as a toiler in the vineyard myself, I now grew irritated that only comedy was deemed to be in need of such support, as if nobody would ever find anything funny unless told it was.

What, logically, was there to be said against taking a sentimental mini-series involving, as they so often seem to, terminal diseases or blokes running off with the woman upstairs, and adding to its crucial moments the sound of sobbing, or Kleenex being blown? Would horror stories, fictional and documentary alike, not benefit from the occasional shriek and retch? Are there not more and more occasions, these days, when a little off-screen heavy breathing would not be entirely inappropriate? Would party political broadcasts not be incalculably enlivened by the odd pre-emptive raspberry?

I think the canning industry could well do themselves a favour here. And since you ask, I seek none of my own: whatever the going rate for donors, it will never be mine. Faced with most television, what I do best is snore, and I can't see much of a market for that.

Labour Party

I wish, this morning, I were chiselling words out literally. Of a granite slab, in the open sleet, with fingers chipped and blue as the stone. But I am not. I am chiselling them out only metaphorically. It is how I generally describe the job of getting words out, because jocularity is a hedge against pretension, and when inquisitive laymen ask me about the nature of the, er, creative process, I smile this shy dismissive smile I have and I say I don't know about any of that, I just climb into the roof of a morning and start chiselling words out. This may sound phony, but if you are a hack and someone asks you how you go about it, there is no way of not sounding phony, and anyway it is like that. Except I do not actually use a chisel.

But Keith actually uses a chisel. When inquisitive laymen ask Keith about the nature of the demolition process, Keith doubtless smiles this shy dismissive smile he has and says I don't know about any of that, I just climb onto the roof of a morning and start chiselling bricks out. That is where he is now, banging away at my chimney stack. And I am level with him, banging away at my wordprocessor. The difference is, I am inside and Keith is outside. From time to time, we glance at one another through the attic window, and when this happens, I type even faster. The words I type are meaningless, and when I have finished typing them, I press the key which deletes them, but Keith doesn't know this, he just thinks I'm working my fingers to the bone.

At least, I hope he does. I even underscore that hope by looking variously morose and frantic. I tear my hair, I pinch the bridge of my nose, I hurl balls of paper into the bin, I swear as noisily as I can. I want Keith to know this writing game is not all beer and skittles, just sitting in the warm and tapping at a keyboard. I want Keith to glance at me and think, look at that poor sod, I may be out here in this sub-zero gale risking life and limb, but at least I am not in there going stark raving mad, what a life, how does he do it, day after day?

I want Joe to think that, too. Joe is the plumber. Joe is downstairs replacing the boiler which will be attached to the new flue after Keith has finished demolishing enough of the chimney to poke the new flue through. Thus, in order for Joe to think that, too, I have to trudge downstairs from time to time, so that Joe can hear me cursing and see me looking morose and frantic. You may think this unnecessary, since Joe is not out on the freezing roof watching me sitting in the warm and tapping at a keyboard, for all Joe knows I might have gone out to work before he arrived and be down the mine right now hewing at the coalface with a canary gasping its last beside me. But I did not go out to work before Joe arrived; when Joe arrived, I answered the door. In my dressing-gown. Which I found it necessary to explain at once by lying to Joe about being up until 5 a.m. typing, why do we kill ourselves, Joe, we only pass this way but once, there has to be more to life than . . .

Then there is all the supine work, which is what hacks have to do in between chiselling. I normally do this in the attic, but if I do so today, Keith will see me, and if I do it downstairs, Joe will see me, and if they see me they will not understand that I am doing some deep thinking. they will think I am doing some deep kipping, so I shall have to do it in the bedroom, and if they chance to catch me at it when they are carrying pipework through, I shall have to say I have this terrible headache, it comes of staring at a bloody VDU all the hours God gave, a lot of writers have to retire early, and no pension to speak of, Keith . . .

They already know it's a very physical job. Manual labour, really. We established this yesterday, at wash-up time. We all used the sink in the kitchen to get the muck off, it's a filthy business, typing, people don't realise, and I went Ow! Ow! and Joe and Keith said what is it, and I said you mean you've never read about Repetitive Strain Injury, it's a very serious wrist complaint you get from typing, some writers end up crippled, and Joe and Keith said getaway, really, dear oh dear.

Why blue collars should make white ones feel guilty, but not vice versa, who can say? It's no good asking me, that

intellectual wossname is all above my head. I just chisel words
out.

Time for a Quick One?

H ere's something you didn't know. Georges Simenon
never had woodworm. The great Walloon was never
infested. Do you still maintain that this little corner shop
of mine trades only in frivolities?

Were I further to point out not only that his waste-disposal
never had a spoon down it, but also that he knew a Chubb 3R35
deadlock nightlatch when he saw one, this would probably be
too much hard fact for you to absorb all at once, you would
almost certainly have to go and lie down, so I shall hold back
for a bit. But be warned: the big stuff is on the way. When it
comes to critical theory, I do not spar. I can go 15 rounds with
the best.

Interim, the scene now shifts to Monday morning, to find me
curled up with Patrick Marnham's new biography, *The Man
Who Wasn't Maigret: A Portrait of Georges Simenon*. I read a
lot of literary biography, you have to if you aspire to be a
novelist, it is the best way of discovering what you need to do in
order to write the sort of books you wish to emulate. I first
committed myself to this 35 years ago, when I read William
Faulkner (people did, then), only to discover that he had jotted
his early masterpieces while working as a trawlerman, coal-
heaver, oil-rigger, steeplejack and various other callings not
readily on tap in the London suburbs, even if you could have
fitted the Archangel run and refurbishing Salisbury spire into the

A-level timetable, so I gave up on being Faulkner and went on to being Hemingway, until I found out that I would have to run through Pamplona doing the thing with the bulls that can give you a wound down there, so then I moved on to being Scott Fitzgerald, because all you had to do was drink, but it did not help me to write *Gatsby*, it just helped me to walk into the furniture, and that is pretty much the way things went with my fictional ambitions over the next three decades, you would be amazed what novelists have to go through, need I remind you that Trollope had to invent the pillarbox in order to fire up his muse?

But then came Monday. I had always admired Simenon – a hundred novels was it? – but I had never known how he had managed it until I read Marnham's book and discovered that Simenon had bedded 10,000 women, even though his wife claimed it was only 1,200 (did they sit down nightly with ready-reckoners and compare lists, did she cry, "I see where you've gone wrong, Georges, you've got that big Irish readhead down twice"?), but it was still enough to get the novels going, and I thought to myself, that's not so difficult, I could do that, especially when I discovered that Georges would often knock off four women in the same afternoon by going up to them in the street, palpating their breasts, and then finding a doorway, it couldn't take that long, you would be back at the typewriter by teatime.

So I put down the book and I ran upstairs to choose a seductive tie, and I splashed on this terrific aftershave I have, and I was just going through the front door when Mr Elias came out of the kitchen I may have told you we are having rebuilt, and he said look at this, and it was a floorboard with a million titchy holes in, and I said what is it, and he said it is woodworm, you are infested, you will have to get Rentokil over, so I had to fix that up and wait in for on-site inspection and early estimate when I could have been out palpating, and that was Monday shot, but I made an early start on Tuesday and nearly got to the garage before Mr Elias caught up and said he could fit the new side door if I went down to Danico and got him a Chubb 3R35 deadlock nightlatch, so I drove to Swiss Cottage and I passed some really fantastic-looking women on the way, many of them conveniently near doorways, but when I got home again Mr Elias said that is the wrong lock, so I drove back to Danico, and I exchanged locks, by which time it was noon, but there was still half a day until Mr Elias said there was a spoon stuck down the waste disposal, and I said can't you do it, and he said do you want this new door in or not, and by the time I had dismantled the waste disposal it was half past two, and I had to write this piece for *The Times*, without even one palpation to inspire me.

Which is how I know that Simenon never had woodworm.

You Are What You Eat

The last thing you want a restaurant to do for you is open up a can of worms. When eating out, you do not require any new complications. You will have quite enough on your plate already, because apart from having to decide what it is you are going to have on your plate, and whether it is going to be quite enough and, furthermore, what it is you are going to have on the plate beside that – a slice, a roll, a crispbread, white, beige, granary, something with fashionable bits in, and, if so, which bits, olive, walnut, fieldmouse? – and what to have in the glass beside your plate, and furthermost, these days, what you are going to have in the glass beside *that* – still, fizzy, French, Highland, Malvern, tap? – apart from all this, I say, there is more than enough to occupy two fraught hours of anyone's bewilderment without having to take on board some fat new codicil to the decision-making process.

There is, for example, rare, medium, charred, there is on or off the bone, there is grated parmesan or not, there is black pepper or not, there are a dozen different mustards, as many different coffees ... and all this ceaselessly bearing down on a brain which began taking heavy punishment the instant it stepped into the place and began to wonder whether or not to check its hat, and, if so, whether to do it before addressing the decision as to which of the 30 tables it wanted to sit at. Who, given all this, would also wish to be faced with deciding how he wanted his lunch killed?

I raise this only because, on Sunday, it was raised for me; to the thinnest of levels, admittedly, but I know a wedge-end when I see one. I had taken my daughter to Gee's, possibly our favourite Oxford restaurant until Sunday came along to slot that "possibly" in, and, having got past the stuff with the hat and the table, we were wrestling with the menu's options, when I said, "I think I'll start with the tuna, but why does it say 'linecaught' in brackets?"

And Victoria rolled her eyes and said, "Because it's more humane than netting, of course. Besides which, dolphins get caught in tuna nets. Would you want to eat a dolphin?"

She had me there. It has long been a rule of mine never to eat anything smarter than I am. Moreover, trained dolphins, I recalled, were rumoured to have fought for the CIA in Vietnam. You would not want to eat an old soldier.

"The fact remains," I said, "that the restaurant is offering me something which they advertise as having been dragged around by its lip. Humane or not, it would never have occurred to me to think about it, had they not brought it up. I shall start with the prawns."

"I wonder how they kill prawns?" said Victoria. "Swat them?"

"Prawns are not killed," I said. "They just die."

"Slowly?"

"I don't know," I said, "the menu doesn't specify. Mind you, since it describes them as King Prawns I suppose it's on the cards that they were individually hanged with a silken rope. I shall have the fettucine instead. The suffering undergone by pasta must be negligible. And after that I'll have the glazed breast of duck."

"I think it ought to say how they killed the duck," said Victoria. "I mean, did they bring it down with a clean shot, or did they just wing it so's the dog could have a bit of fun finishing it off? Or was it the sort they corner in farmyards and strangle? No wonder it's glazed."

"Stop this," I said. "I know where it's going. Youthful sarcasm and I are old friends. Any minute now, we shall be in the middle of the one about political rectitude as viewed by the middle-aged ostrich. Do not get me wrong: I am perfectly happy to eat a friend of the earth who has been bumped off by topically acceptable means, but I don't see why I have to have it rammed down my throat."

"As it were. How about the rib of beef? Who knows, we might find out that it was seen off by El Cordobes after putting up a damned good show. It may have gone the way it would have chosen. You'd like that."

I looked at the waiter.

"You see what you've started," I said.

FEBRUARY

Smoke Without Fire

A day or so ago, I bought a pack of Silk Cut, peeled its Cellophane, flipped its lid, plucked its foil off, and gasped.

Doesn't surprise me, the smug will cry, smoking seriously damages health, the poor sod cannot even open a pack these days without the effort of putting a major drain on his guttering constitution; but you are wrong, at least in the matter of the gasp. It proceeded not from exhaustion, but from bliss; for there, nestled flat against the fags, one thin edge peeping over the packet's rim with all the heady titillation of yore, was a cigarette card. I drew it out. It showed a carving-knife addressing a taut purple thread, but instead of the former bisecting the latter, it was the thread which cut deep into the blade.

Oh joy, I thought, I know what this is, this is a conjuring trick, this will amaze my family and amuse my friends, I had a series of these once, an aeon ago, how to take an egg from your ear, how to push a pencil through a brick wall – well, I say series, I had 47, David Collingwood had the other three, but he wanted six "Kings of Speed" for them, including Rudolf

Caracciola and Raymond Mays, nobody else in the world had those, they had cost me half a set of luminous dinosaur skeletons, shine a bedclothed torch on them, then switch it off, and you were back in the Mesozoic era, more or less – so I turned over the new cigarette card to find out how the trick was done.

It was a different kind of trick. The instructions said: "There are 20 different Silk Cut advertisements in these specially marked packs. Collect all 20 and claim £5." Aren't you glad you live in 1993? Who'd want to know how to take an egg from his ear, when he could have a fiver instead?

Anyone who had ever savoured the Golden Age of Pasteboard is who. Forget nostalgia: education is the issue here. Care to test me? Ask me to draw *Tyrannosaurus rex*; I see him now, shimmering against the upper bedsheet, and I could jot him to the life, or at any rate the bones. Invite me to rattle off the kings and queens of England in sequence, and I shall throw in 200 words on each for good measure. Beg me for the RAC-rating of the chain-driven Frazer-Nash, or the top speed of the Isotta Fraschini Monterosa, and you will not see an eyelid bat. Need Wally Hammond's Test average, W.E. Gladstone's dates, the Dragon Rapide's wing-span, the *Mauretania*'s displacement? Just ask. Alternatively, why not sidle up to any contemporary ten-year-old, enquire of him the height of New Zealand's tallest mountain, and see how close he gets?

Nor was my education at the hands of Capstan and Woodbine purely academic. Cigarette cards were the set text in the University of Life. A whole generation learned to dance from a few square inches of Victor Sylvester, and when, today, besotted women press their lips against my foxtrotting ear and ask how it is that I have the reverse telemark off to such perfection, I tell them it is all because my old man was a smoker. Similarly, when opponents stand flatfooted as my cross-court backhand volley rockets past them, and cry: "My God, that is just how Fred Perry used to play it!", I simply smile and murmur, "I know, I know".

Family values? Nothing encouraged parental respect like fag-cards: the father or mother who was in a position to withhold

Joe Louis from a child who already had 49 "Giants of the Ring" could get a lawn mown, a deaf relative visited, a room tidied, with no more than a nod. As for making our own entertainment, dear God, we made our own *books*! Somewhere I have the albums still, umpteen titchy encyclopaedias containing a sizeable whack of all I have ever learnt.

Pity the modern infant: his notorious ignorance and unruliness is down to nothing more than the disappearance of the cigarette card. Since schools are no longer places where pupils can convene to swap and pore, no wonder illiteracy and truancy are rife. That is what infuriates me about the chance Silk Cut have thrown away; what astonishes me is that they did not appreciate what a trump the card could be. With the government under the cosh to both ban cigarette advertising and improve education standards, here, surely, was a deal waiting to be done. Here was the swap of swaps, and Silk Cut have blown it.

Lost For Words

While you are staring at this, I shall be staring at an insurance claim form. I know that that is what I shall be doing, because it is what I have been doing for some time past, and it is what I shall be continuing to do for some time to come; I have stopped doing it now only for long enough to tell you what it is I am doing, because it is important for you to know. Important, that is, to me. It doesn't matter a damn to you. You haven't just waved goodbye to a million pounds.

If that's what it was. I have no way of assessing exactly what it was I waved goodbye to, which is why my days are spent staring at a claim form. Nor did I wave goodbye to it personally, since I was a thousand miles away when it went; if I had not been, it would not have gone, because the bastard who last week put a jemmy to the shutters of my little French bolt-hole and sheared off its little French bolts would have been working his night shift at some other, unoccupied, target.

What, then, was nicked, and why do I not have the remotest idea what it was worth? Well, what was nicked was the familiarly nickable, a television set, a VCR, radios, binoculars, phones, a few other bits and bobs, and a computer. Hang on, you will mutter, what is he going on about, that's never a million quid, he must know what that stuff's worth, he is a man of the world, why doesn't he just jot it on his claim form and bang it off to his insurers, so that we can all get some peace? That is because you do not know what was on the computer.

For the past year, I have been cobbling a novel. And do not ascribe that description to the bogus humility with which hacks pretend to dismiss their worth: cobbling is precisely what I have been doing. Since subsistence duties leave me no time for fiction, it is only when I take French leave of them that I am able to knock out the odd narrative chunk and nail it on the end of the one I did on the previous trip; or possibly on the front of it, because you can do that, with a computer. Thus, by these spatchcock means, the novel had lurched its way to some 20,000 words, many of them different, but all of them inscribed on the hard disk of my Apple Macintosh. Which, a week ago, fell onto the back of a lorry. My God, you cry, I thought we said he was a man of the world, did he not have the sense to copy this book of his onto back-up floppies? Yes, he did, and he also had the sense to place the floppies next to his computer so that he would know where to find them; for which the bastard with the jemmy will have been extremely grateful, since you do not wish to waste precious time on broken and entered premises poking around for the box of disks which will make a nicked computer even more saleable.

To whom? Need you ask? This is Provence we're talking about: by day the cicadas are inaudible in the rattle of typewriters, by night the glow-worms are upstaged by the flicker of VDUs, for the hills are alive with the sound of expatriate hacks shrieking that they could be the next Peter Mayle, all it takes is one good idea. Well, there is one good idea on the loose there, now, and when I reflect on the obvious customer my thief will seek for an Anglophone word-processor, my heart plummets bootwards. The recipient could well find himself sitting on a goldmine.

Just how good an idea it is, mind, I cannot know, which is why I can't fill in the claim form box about the compensation I can't assess. Are we talking hardback blockbuster, tabloid serial rights, gilt-embossed transglobal paperback? Are we talking Spielberg, John Thaw, T-shirts, arcade video spin-offs, eponymous fried-chicken outlets? Or are we talking remainder shelves, dog-ears, wonky piano legs?

I may never know, but if I do, I may not want to. Because while I don't have the stomach for a fresh start, whoever inherits the computer won't need one, and if there turns out to be a million in it, it'll be his. Unless, that is, I can sue it off him, which is why I began by telling you how important you were. I don't get much time for reading, and I need your help: should you one day find yourself snuggling into your airline seat with a bestseller beginning: "At 4.20 on the chill morning of January 9, Her Majesty Queen Elizabeth II slipped a .38 Smith & Wesson into her reticule, and left Balmoral via the laundry-chute", tip me the wink.

Table Talk

Dear Barrington Hill, I know you will forgive my writing to you out of the blue, since I do so in reply to yours out of the blue of the 25th ult; but dare I hope that you will also forgive my explaining to the general reader that you are not, as your name might beguile them into imagining, either a stop on the Northern Line or a little-known Civil War skirmish, but the general manager of American Express? For general readers are notoriously ill-informed, which indeed is why you wrote to me in the first place. You wish to rectify this; at least, in 850 cases.

Mahogany cases, at that.

You will recall that your letter offered me "the greatest writing of the last 3,000 years, housed in a beautiful revolving bookcase specially commissioned by American Express, each one hand-embossed with the initials of the purchasing cardmember." You did this because, as you were sure I would appreciate, great writing is the foundation of our civilisation. You then enquired whether I myself sometimes wished I were better-read – "when, for example, someone at a party refers to something as Orwellian or Kafkaesque, or when a business acquaintance refers to the economic theories of Adam Smith or Keynes".

Barrington, you ask a straight question and you deserve a straight answer. Certainly, I sometimes wish I were better-read; but never when someone at a party refers to something as Orwellian or Kafkaesque. When someone at a party does that, I wish only that I were better-plastered. If the business acquaintance beside him chips in with a pithy gobbet or two from *The Wealth of Nations*, I wish only to move on, in the hope that the lissom redhead steadying herself against the china cabinet is looking for a lift home.

Nor does my heart go pit-a-pat at your sly suggestion that "there's a positive use of such knowledge as well: the opportunity to enliven your conversation with the thoughts and wisdom of great thinkers". For we are both men of the world, Barrington, and when I glance at your list of 130 authors – Euclid, Tacitus, Archimedes and the rest – may I not be forgiven for wondering how far over a lissom redhead, say, would be bowled over by the latest gossip concerning specific gravity?

Never mind. Let us not be crass about all this, nor even pause to wonder how we came to be selected from millions for the chance to join that exclusive band at whom this limited edition is aimed – did extensive research come up with a roll of Britain's 850 deadest conversationalists? – but address the offer's unsettling nub.

The free mahogany bookcase.

The bookcase is very important. In your leafleture, Barrington, while there is only one list of your great authors, there are three photographs of your great bookcase. Indeed, it has a brochure all its own, showing "the remote corner of Suffolk where small flintstone cottages resound to the time-honoured noise of woodworking". Tap-tap, whirr-whirr, buff-buff, go the craftsmen, plying adze and gimlet selflessly in the service of the cardholding illiterate. Nor is this any old bookcase: it revolves – "a Victorian concept which brought to the drawing-room the books they needed for regular access, as opposed to the volumes which merely gathered dust in the library".

Now, I do not carp at this: a man has to know where he can put his finger on Montesquieu or Ptolemy. He could go barmy, sitting alone, unable to recall Wittgenstein's favourite rib-tickler. But if he is not alone? Here, Barrington, is my carp: for I note that your bookcase does not merely revolve, it moves. It has four castors. It can be pulled around the room by any keen conversationalist. Sturdy as it is, it could even be towed behind his car. Any day now, each of 850 cardmembers will be in a position to follow the rest of us about, tugging in his gabbling wake Thucydides, Plotinus, Heidegger, Brecht . . .

There will be no escape from the enlivened conversation lurking in that bookcase. The poor sap will believe it'll do nicely. God help us all, Barrington, he won't leave home without it.

Deep Waters Run Still

I had done the easy bit. I had dug out the first channel, I had laid 20 metres reinforced suction hose, PVC, @ £3.95 per metre, I had affixed thereto one gate-valve, brass @ £5.90, I had filled the first channel in, I had dug the second channel, parallel, I had laid 20 metres 3-core cable, rubber, @ £1.20 per metre, I had affixed thereto one Duraplug 13-amp cable connector, waterproof, @ £13.90, one powerbreaker socket, ditto, @ £24.45, and one BWG Multi-Switch MS2, @ £32.90, I had filled the second channel in, I had made good and removed all rubbish from site as per mine of the 19th inst., I had broken four nails, finger, @ considerable personal anguish, I had driven back and forth to the aquatic centre twice and to the cashpoint three times and now I had to drive to the aquatic centre a third time, because I had done the easy bit, and the moment had come when I had to do the hard bit.

I had to put something on the end of all this. I had to buy a statue with a hole in it.

This was even harder than burying the fish, and that was hard enough.

When you have had the same fish for 20 years, give or take the odd heron raid and catsnack, a bond is forged. From their side, mind, that bond is called fishfood, but from yours it is about seigneurial obligation and the love that asks no questions. Thus, when a couple of weeks ago I returned from France to find the fish not swimming but floating, having popped their fins *nem con* for reasons still unknown, proper obsequies were called for. You cannot just bung them on the compost heap, or bury them any old where to have their tiny spines reappearing like Banquo every time the geraniums have to be taken up, you have to find a last resting-place, preferably one near a rustic bench where you can sit and stare at it, reflecting that the days of fish are but as grass.

So I did that, and then I drained the pond; for life must go on, but it was patently not going to go on in the pond as it stood, you had only to look at it, never mind point the nostril; the Creature from the Black Lagoon wouldn't last five minutes in it. After I had drained it, I went to see my friend at the aquatic centre for new weed, snails, lilies, fish, all that, and my friend said what's all this about, then, and after I had told him, he dried his shoulder and remarked, "I've said it before, and I'll say it again, what you need is an ornamental fountain. Oxygenates the water, you can go on holiday with a clear conscience, also makes a wonderful feature, a conversation piece, plus this very nice trickling sound, it gives you a different class of pond altogether."

At which juncture, he slid expertly aside to allow me to take in the serried concrete ranks behind him.

"We have the biggest range there is," he said, "we have the Cherub Trio, we have the Lotus Flower, we have the Frog, we have the Goose Boy plus up to four Geese, we have the Boy on Dolphin, Lorelei, Niobe, we have the Mermaid, either Topless or With Tresses, we have the Leaping Frog, the Lilypad and Frog, we have Peter Pan, or there's the Brussels Boy for the lighter touch, it comes out of his thingy, possibly not to everyone's taste, but a very popular line, we have the basic Buddha and also Ho Tai the Laughing Buddha, we have . . ."

"It's hard to as it were, you know, see them *in situ*," I said.

"Tell you what," he said, "lay all the services, it'll give you a bit of time to think, then come back when you've decided."

So I did all that; except decide. It is not easy, staring at a Cricklewood garden and wondering whether it is better suited to a Jolly Turtle or a Cherub Trio. You can become fountain-drunk, you can find visions sidling into your head of a Versailles restocked with four hundred Brussels Boys all peeing at one another.

But I did the hard thing at last. I bought Ho Tai the Laughing Buddha @ £62.50. I fitted him up to the twin services, and I filled the pond, and I switched him on. But the water did not gush out of his mouth; it gushed out of his ear.

At the time of writing, I still haven't decided whether to unbolt him again and fiddle with him. Whatever else he is, you would, if you saw him, have to admit he is a conversation piece.

Nobody looking at him would be able to resist asking why the hell he is laughing.

Does It Hurt to Be Polite?

How are we to handle the New Intimacy? It invites those capitals, for it is not merely a vogue, it is a movement. Indeed, its acolytes no doubt describe it as a philosophy: management summons a staff kitted out in chirpy new uniforms, nothing too dominant of course, nothing sartorially hectoring, an initialled tie perhaps, a logo brooch, a corporate cufflink, and declares: "From today, here at Happitrash Transglobal Novelties plc, our new philosophy is founded on intimacy. The public is our playgroup! The customer is our chum! Make one another feel good! Go out there and hug!"

You know the rest. Once, we were sir and modom, you and I, and formality was our guide and our protection. We all, seller and buyer alike, knew where we were. Of course, growing acquaintance might allow us to elasticise that rigidity, we might have come to know one another as Mr Warburton of Goods Pending and Mr Coren of Cricklewood; even, in the fullness of time, as Syd and Alan, though time, however full, would also have to have been given a hefty nudge by circumstance, e.g. running into one another in the four-bob ring at Kempton, raising our trilbies to one another's good lady wives, and asking one another whether we fancied Lester in the 3.15, that sort of thing. But intimacy was never summarily pre-empted. That would never have done, because it would have made a professional relationship impossible. We would, in short, not have known where we stood.

142

Yet this is precisely what has now happened. I telephone, let us say, British Gas. British Gas says: "Hallo, Julie speaking, thank you for calling, how may I help you?" I, poised to give some nameless ratbag an earful, where are your bloody fitters, then, I have been stuck here for three days, etc, cannot. The New Intimacy requires me to say, "Hallo, Julie, thank you for answering, my name is Coren, well, Alan actually, I have this problem, just a little one, hardly a problem at all, really ..." I am, God help me, chatty. Some time thus passes before Julie says, "That is not my area, Colin, let me pass you to Trevor, would you mind holding, just for a moment?" at which point William Tell comes on with his overture in tow, occasionally interrupted by a soloist with a tin glottis who sings, "Hallo, thank you for calling British Gas, you are being held in a queue, our staff will be with you as soon as possible", until such time as that member is with me, saying, "Hallo, Trevor speaking, thank you for calling, how may I ..." which goes on for a bit until we are forced to the conclusion that Trevor may not be the person I need, so I ask Trevor to pass me back to Julie, because Julie has all my details, but Trevor says, "Which Julie was that?" and I cannot tell him. Up against a skyscraper packed with Julies, I have to ring off and start again, but I do not get one of the Julies this time, I get one of the Trishes. But when I ask the Trish I get what her surname is in case one of the Trevors wants to put me back to her, I am told she is sorry, she is not allowed to give that information.

Thus is the whistle blown on the New Intimacy. It is entirely bogus, designed to make us feel close, but in fact making us feel more remote than when we were sir and modom, able to say what we wanted to say, and being told Mr Warburton's name if we asked for it. If something is not done to stay this development, pretty soon we shall be ringing up to hear: "Hallo, Julie speaking, thank you for calling, how are the children, what is your birth sign, isn't it hot, have you had your holidays yet, do you know Trevor, how may ..." and we shall then be remoter than ever.

Worse yet. I see from the Passenger's Charter that all BR staff are now required to wear badges with their Christian names clearly displayed; so how long can it be before a codicil to the Citizen's Charter demands the rest of us follow suit? Mark me, this entire island may very soon resemble a Milwaukee sales conference, with all of us grinning vacuously and peering at one another's lapels.

And who could doubt that the unprecedented naming of the head of MI6 wasn't directly down to the New Intimacy? Ring up, and I bet you'll hear: "Hallo, Colin speaking, thank you for calling the Secret Service, how may I help you?"

Do Dilly-Dally on the Way

You will groan (and who could blame you?) to recall my obsessive search, *passim*, for a Cricklewood hero. So let me lift your spirits: the search is over. After today, you will hear no more of it. Even if other local prodigies turn up as unexpectedly as this one, they shall not test your patience. I am satisfied, now, to let the matter rest, along with the blessed remains of a paragon whose ineffable *rightness* for me and Cricklewood sets her immovably above any putative contender.

Heroine, then. And those remains lie not 200 yards from my very gate, though I didn't know this until yesterday, despite having passed them umpteen times on as many short cuts through the cemetery at the top of the road. But yesterday's was a long cut: as I negotiated the wonky crosses, February suddenly did what February suddenly does, so, lacking an umbrella, I shot under a maple tree to wait for it to stop doing it. I was not alone, for that is the way it is in graveyards, but I did not immediately spot who was beside me, because the moss lay thick in the chisellings. It was only when I thought I saw what I subsequently knew I had that I ran my finger down the grooves to ream them out, and read: "In loving memory of Marie Lloyd, born February 12, 1870, died October 7, 1922."

Even then, and even as the fingers trembled, I couldn't be sure it was her – *that* her, I mean. And then I read the mottled verse beneath.

> Tired she was, and she wouldn't show it.
> Suffering she was, and hoped we didn't know it.
> But He who loved her knew, and, understanding all,
> Prescribed long rest, and gave the final call.

Who else could it be? You could hear her singing that first couplet, and anyone who knew anything about Marie Lloyd knew the significance of the second, because she died in the middle of her act at the Edmonton Empire, in the middle, indeed, of "One of the Ruins that Cromwell Knocked About a Bit". Furthermore, she died because she had been knocked about more than a bit by her swine of a third husband, jockey Bernard Dillon, and (since, even with all that, irony remained unsatisfied) she died staggering as if drunk, but because the song required her to stagger as if drunk, the audience laughed and cheered while she terminally tottered. I do not know if He, understanding all, fixed it so that the last sound she heard was of an enraptured music hall, you would have to ask a believer, but there have been worse ways to go.

When the shower eased, I walked across to the cemetery office, and Cliff Green, who runs it, took down the book for 1922, and showed me an entry no less apt in its macabre comedy than the final call itself, in that Matilda Alice Victoria Dillon, known as Marie Lloyd, had been interred 12 ft down, for £52 2s 0d, and that her mother Matilda Wood had been interred above her (9 ft) in 1931, and her father above *her* (7 ft) in 1940, and her sister above *him* (4 ft) in 1968, and just as I had seemed to hear her sing before, now I seemed to hear her laugh, and I knew that laugh, I had heard it countless times on the wheezy old 78 I replay whenever I need a little of what I fancy to do me good, and Mr Green said there was one more thing I might like

145

to know, which is that both gates of Fortune Green Cemetery had been opened only once, and that was on October 12, 1922.

It was the biggest funeral they had ever had, and they had been compelled to close those same gates an hour before the burial, because all three local police stations couldn't provide enough constables to control the weeping mob, and it was no good drafting in volunteers because, as you know, you can't trust a special like the old-time coppers.

Marie Lloyd, however, despite the dilly-dallying of the cortège from her house in Woodstock Road as the result of so many wreaths being flung at the cars by grieving bystanders that the half-mile journey took almost an hour, did, at last, find her way home, and I rejoice that it's just a step across the road from mine. Tonight I shall put on "A Little of What You Fancy", turn up the volume, and open the windows for her to hear.

And if you remind me I'm not a believer, I shall, like Marie, just wink the other eye.

MARCH

Something for the Weekend

Oh God, a snowdrop has appeared outside my window. Well, probably a snowdrop; could be an anaemic crocus, I am not a man to run to with floral queries, horses for courses, but whatever it is, it is a harbinger, that much I do know. It has shoved itself through the lawn with an announcement. The heart sinks. Any day now, I shall begin receiving letters with rural postmarks, the general thrust of which will be to invite me to rise up and come away, for, lo, the winter is past, the rain is over and gone, the flowers appear on the earth, the time of the singing of the birds is come, and the voice of the turtle is heard in the land.

The turtle will want me and the wife to join it for a weekend in the country. The turtle either lives in the country, or owns a weekend bolt-hole there, as the result of either of which it has to have company or it will go barmy. That is not to say that it isn't a worthy turtle, generous, gregarious, convivial, hospitable to a fault; many turtles, indeed, buy places in the country primarily because they wish not merely to entertain more chums (*sic*) than can comfortably be accommodated in titchy town-houses, but

149

also to entertain them more liberally. For you cannot chuck another log into the inglenook of a smokeless Belgravia mews, nor dance the Gay Gordons the length and breadth of a Hampstead flat, nor take your horse for a brisk canter over Notting Hill and return to suck up Bollinger with 300 absolutely sooper neighbours on a Kensington balcony, while the ox turns, crisping, in the microwave.

The fact that, at the thought of country weekends, my heart aches and a drowsy numbness pains my sense thus has nothing whatever to do with the turtles, who are wonderful hosts. It has everything to do with me, who is a terrible guest.

I travel well, but, unless I am able to command the environment to which I have travelled, I transplant badly. Dispatch me to my carefully-selected hotel, knowing what I have planned for the weekend and with whom and in which clothes, and that there are staff on hand to satisfy my whims in return for folding money, and, come Friday evening, I shall let Cricklewood dwindle in my wing-mirror with an optimistic heart. I shall know where I stand, and, more important, where I shall be standing later.

I shall know I shall not be standing in a corridor at 3 a.m. between my room and the bathroom it turns out not to have *en suite*, inadequately clad in my wife's peignoir because I did not bring my dressing-gown, and not knowing (a) which of these doors has a bathroom behind it, (b) whether my host's Alsatian, which has just materialised at the far end of the corridor, had a good enough sniff of me when I arrived to distinguish me from a prowling transvestite wondering which door conceals the family silver, or (c) if not, whether it would be better to stand stock still or run like hell.

Even at 6 a.m., the scenario would be little better. I have woken with a sandpaper throat, thanks, first, to being forced to shout off-key round a piano for some hours and, second, to drinking in a corner for some more hours to eradicate my previous embarrassment, and what I am now desperate for is a cuppa, but where do they keep the tea, where do they keep the sugar, the milk must be in the fridge, yes it is, but, bloody hell, it is on the floor, now, why are the *outsides* of milk bottles always wet, and, oh look, the Alsatian has heard the crash, a prowling transvestite is stealing the family's food ...

Turtles don't invariably keep an Alsatian, mind. They do not need one if they have a burglar alarm, wired to alert not only the sleeping household to the fact that a drunken cross-dresser has just walked through a photo-electric beam, but also the local constabulary who, with any luck, will arrive any minute now with their own Alsatian.

Not that a terrible guest requires such disasters in order to have a terrible time. He may have woken at 6 a.m. and done nothing more than stare out of the window for three hours, wondering what time the house has breakfast, finally creeping downstairs to discover that it has it at 7.30 and that Mrs Daily, who does for the turtles, has just finished shaking the tablecloth out. True, there is a stiff rasher of cold bacon left in a frying-pan, but there is also an Alsatian looking at it.

Upon returning to his room so that he can inform his wife that she was absolutely right, countryfolk do indeed breakfast early, sorry, he sees (a) that she is not there, and (b) that, from the window, the turtles and all their guests are briskly marching across a paddock towards a distant wood. Knowing that a good guest would have been of their number, the terrible guest attempts to make amends by hurtling off in pursuit.

The paddock, up close, proves to have the consistency of the Somme salient, but it is now too late to go back and ask Mrs Daily whether the turtles keep wellies for guests who forgot to put them in their boot, he is in mud stepp'd in so far that, should he wade no more, returning were as tedious as go o'er. He eventually squelches up to the party at the exact moment they are entering the wood, and thus poised to begin excitedly identifying things. "Good God, isn't that *Argybargy con-dominium* over there, how incredible, it's only March, oh, look, what a splendid example of Old Man's Bum, down there near that enormous clump of *Copious mucus*, I've never seen such a remarkable ..."

Others, meanwhile, prefer to search the skies: "It can't be, where are my field glasses, yes, by heaven, it is, it's Snorkel's

Falcon, there must be a colony of bandy voles round here, they're the only prey a Snorkel's ..."

The terrible guest can contribute nothing whatever to this. Raised in an environment where anything attempting to grow through a crack in the patio fell to the blow lamp before it could burgeon into identifiability, and unable to distinguish between a sparrow and a starling unless they happen to be lying dead together so that one can be seen to be larger than the other, he can do nothing but pray that some litter-lout has ambled this way and given him the opportunity to cry, "I say, isn't that a Mars wrapper?" before anyone else spots it.

Everyone now romps home for lunch, duly banging on about country air and appetites, none of them more ravenous than the breakfastless guest. And lunch is rather special.

You can tell this right away from all the nudging and winking by the turtles. Because lunch is one of Mrs Daily's famous game pies, and Mr Daily is, well, no names, no pack drill, a bit of a poacher, ha-ha, don't ask what's in it, just tuck in. The pie is the size of a suitcase. Beneath his triangular slab, the terrible guest can see strange rhomboid chunks, arcane organs, little limbs. Is this Mrs Daily's famous gull-and-weasel, perhaps, her famous toe-and-bladder, her ...

After lunch, while his wife helps with the washing-up by putting everything away in cupboards from which they have subsequently to be removed by people who know where they go, the terrible guest can think of no other way of doing his bit than by asking whether anyone wants anything from the village. A turtle cries: "Stout fellow, as a matter of fact, we're out of cumin, there's none in our village, but try the grocer in Courtney Walsh, and if he's shut, there's one by the church in Curtley Ambrose." Some hours later, the terrible guest finds himself in Stokely Carmichael, trying to buy an Ordnance Survey map. He does not succeed.

It is dark when he gets back. Everybody is in the bath, except the Alsatian. The terrible guest needs a large one. In a hotel, he would ring a bell, and a large one would instantly appear, flanked by cashews and little onions. Where, though, do the turtles keep the booze? And should he just help himself? The

Alsatian thinks not. The guest tries a cupboard, the Alsatian tries a bark, a turtle appears, in a towel, and says: "Shut up, Radar! Were you after something, old son?" He gives the guest the glass of water he asks for, and goes out again.

Never mind. As soon as everyone has vacated the bathrooms, he will have a nice cold bath to empty unused, and then there will be dinner. He can smell fish. Who knows, Mr Daily may well have caught a few choice gudgeon, possibly a fat frog or two. And after dinner, 50 lovely local people are coming over to the turtles' renovated barn for square-dancing to the talented Daily Trio.

Western clothes, old son, stetsons, cowboy boots, kerchiefs, usual gear. Oh God, didn't you get our note? How terrible!

Still No Flies Undone

I have a plant, and it won't eat. Not only will it not swallow, it won't even chew. Indeed, when you come right down to it, I have no evidence that, since it took up residence, it has actually tried biting anything.

It has been here a week. It came to a dinner party – not for plants, for people – but I did not immediately remove its gift-swaddling since there were prior social incumbencies, and anyway, it would only be a cyclamen, it is always a cyclamen, but when everyone had gone again, I saw that the label said: *Dionaea muscipula* (Venus Fly Trap).

As plants go, it wasn't up to much, you couldn't see where Venus came in, it was hardly more than a spray of skinny stalks dangling over the edge of the pot, each ending in a fronded jaw, but the label said it was "an appealing novelty plant", which made it sound like something that opened the second half at the Hackney Empire, so I put it on a window-sill and went to bed, quite chipper about the whole affair. Since the cat died in 1988, I had not had a pet. Never mind one in show business.

In the morning, there were no flies on it. This did not bother me, for ours are not particularly fly-blown premises, and besides, the thing might have eaten before it set off the previous night: although I knew little of *Dionaea muscipula*, I assumed that it was more intelligent than the average plant (a cyclamen hasn't the first idea how to catch a square meal), and that it would therefore not have undertaken a journey without first gobbling a little something to tide it over.

When, however, it ate nothing all that day, I grew concerned; I had left the window open, the spring was warm, there were flies about, bugs, gnats, ladybirds, but each little jaw lay open and empty, which, according to *Britannica*, they wouldn't be if my pet had eaten: the relevant jaw would have snapped shut to form a spiny cage, enabling the fortunate owner to watch an insect being slowly ingested. That was its novelty; quite how appealing you would find it would rather depend on whether you thought watching a fly getting sucked flat was better than watching an inferior juggler fall off his monocycle, but I was game to give it a go, especially as I had been rather taken by *Britannica's* further news that it was a member of the Sundew family from North Carolina, and suddenly I saw them all, Belle Sundew, Rhett Sundew, Robert E. Sundew, I saw the Old Sundew Place, the darkies strumming, the mockingbirds hooting, the family rocking on the verandah, digesting flies.

Three days, however, brought no change, even after I managed to swat a fly (a thing I thought I should no longer have to do, now there was a professional in the house) and tweezer it gently into one of the plant's gaping jaws. The jaw did not ungape. Did my pet, perhaps, not savour carrion? *Britannica* not saying, I sped to Waterstone with £10.99, sped back with Davidson's *Unusual Houseplants*, and learned that, on the contrary, "when flies are not plentiful, the Venus Fly Trap may be fed with minute pieces of fish".

What a versatile little fellow! Without pausing to speculate on how it could have developed this taste for seafood, I opened a can of sardines, and gave it a morsel. But even as a Venus Fish Trap, it remained inert. And thus, inevitably, guilt crept in. It was off its tucker because it did not like me. It wished it was in Dixie. I did not know what I had done, but, worse, I did not know what to do either. You couldn't bin it, it wasn't a bunch of daffs, it dwelt in that no man's land between vegetable and animal, it would be like binning Lassie, it might even be an offence, the RSPCA would axe the door, I should be banned for life from keeping another pot-plant, vegetable rights activists would aerosol my fence, but what was the option, were there special vets, must I sit with it in some waiting-room alongside weeping freaks whose sea-anemones were on the blink, whose pitcher-plants felt low?

So I rang Kew, and they were, as always, solicitude itself; they faxed me a membership form for the Carnivorous Plant Society, only nine quid to join, but better than that, it is a reg. charity, No 281423; which is why, since you have been wondering, you're reading this. We at the CPS need you: dig deep, give generously. Or we'll send a triffid round.

Flame Is the Spur

It stands to reason, as Worzel Gummidge used to say in the good old days when a scarecrow was a scarecrow, that the faster things change, the faster nostalgia will burgeon in the voids the changes leave. And so rapidly do things change now that by Tuesday, Monday can quite easily seem a good old day.

Before long, no doubt, we shall find ourselves, at around 3 p.m., looking back wistfully at a good old morning, and soon after that we shall probably dab our eyes at the memory of that good old minute which disappeared for ever half an hour before.

Today I went down to my local video-rental shop on West End Green. It wasn't there. What was there was a blackened ruin. Stunned, I stood and trembled, like Vivian Leigh before the remains of Tara, waiting for some faithful old retainer to run from the reeking rubble crying: "Oh, Massa, Massa, de ole video store done burned down, dat Gen'l Sherman done torched de entiah stock!", but nobody came, so I pulled myself together and went next door to enquire. A not unreasonable move, given that next door is the West Hampstead Fire Station, and if they didn't know, who would? Getting it out of them, mind, might be a bit tricky, there could well be a deal of mutual embarrassment to be hurdled, the fire brigade would not, after all, have had to do much to be on the scene, sticking a hose out of one window and into another ought to have done it, they wouldn't even have had to slide down their pole.

"It is being investigated," said the fireman. "We have reason to suspect an accelerator may have been employed." He paused; the pause of the insider. "An accelerator is the term we use to describe a device."

"A tin of petrol, as it were?" I offered.

"It is being investigated," repeated the fireman, and went back to polishing his appliance, because you can never tell when you might have to drive somewhere. Not all fires break out next door.

"Nearest video place is in Mill Lane," said the man in the grocer's, because, though my heart was heavy, life had to go on. I thus arrived at the door of The Video Store. A plaque on this door said: "Multiple Rental Retailer of the Year 1991". I went in. It was not like my dear old incinerated Plug Inn, it did not have an owner's baby gurgling in its pushchair, nor an owner's mum cooking out back, it did not have an owner's cat stropping itself against the till, it had anodised shelving and computers, and when I asked if *Empire of the Sun* was in stock the manager said he would have to see two documents, e.g. gas bill and bank

156

statement, before I could be entered on the membership computer, would I fill in this form stating name, address, birthdate, profession, etc, and indicate in the box provided whether I wanted Supercover Tape Damage Protection for life, only £5?

I enquired, and he slid me a leaflet inviting me to guess what a videotape cost. "£5? £10? £20? No, more like £80, suppose it was eaten by pets or children, stood on, jumped on, chewed up by your VCR? Fear not! Ritz in its usual inventive market-leading ways has the solution."

"Ritz?" I said. "It says The Video Store outside."

"Taken over by Ritz last year," said the manager. "Ritz is a chain of 1,000 outlets. A wholly-owned subsidiary of City-vision. Or was."

"Was?"

"Ritz has just been taken over by Blockbusters," said the manager, "but we've not got the wossname, documentation, yet."

I signed, and walked home to dig out my gas bill and bank statement, and few crossing my path would have guessed that I was crying on the inside, since who would imagine we should one day feel nostalgic for the passing of the corner video shop, its charm, its innocence, its intimacy, its funny little ways? For passing it patently is, whether by molotov cocktail or takeover, or in some cases, perhaps, a mixture of both, to be replaced by megaglomerates who view the customer as some degenerate credit-unworthy madman jumping up and down on a video already half-eaten by his horrible offspring.

When I go back to collect my membership card, I shall not take out *Empire of the Sun*. Instead, I shall see if they've got *Casablanca*. I'd like to hear Sam play "As Time Goes By" again.

Clippings File

If you have a toenail clipper attached to your watch-chain, may I invite you to remove it from your waistcoat pocket and have a look at it? It might well create a bond between us.

I accept that there may not be many of us to have that bond created between. Few men wear waistcoats, let alone watch-chains, and of the handful that do, it is impossible to estimate how many keep a toenail clipper on the non-watch end. As for my female readership, who do not wear watch-chains at all, God alone knows where they keep their toenail clippers. Even in 1993, there are still some things that men do not ask women.

As a matter of fact, I do not wear a watch-chain either. My toenail clipper is still in the box I bought it in, yesterday. The bond I mentioned would be created solely on the basis of the brand of clipper, not on the fact that mine was on a watch-chain. I just thought yours might be. I just thought you might have read the tiny leaflet which came with your toenail clipper and said to yourself, hallo, that sounds like a good idea.

My new toenail clipper is called a Theta. I cannot be sure how the manufacturers arrived at the name, but as I know two things about the Greeks' eighth letter, I am assuming the explanation lies with one of them. The first thing I know is that in ancient Greece, on the ballots used in voting upon a sentence of life or death, the letter theta stood for death. Unable to imagine what this has to do with pedicures, I am assuming that the manufacturers went for the other thing I know about the letter theta, which is that it looks like a toenail.

I took some care in choosing the Theta. It is the type of clipper made as a pair of little crescent jaws activated by a swivelling lever. You place the jaws on the chosen nail, you press the lever, and the end of your nail flies across the room (unless, again, you have read the tiny leaflet; but I shall come to that later). Now, with inferior examples, what can happen is that the lever snaps before the toenail does; this is what happened with my previous clipper, which is why I took some care, yesterday, in choosing a superior one. Just how superior I didn't know until I read the tiny leaflet: "The Theta", it preened, "has a unique clip for conveniently affixing to your keyring or watch-chain."

I thought about this for a bit. Then I put a waistcoat on, and, in lieu of a chain, strung a piece of cord between the pockets and affixed thereto the Theta, by its unique clip. It was not convenient at all. I count myself relatively lissom, but no matter what contortion I attempted, I could not get clipper and toenail within a foot of one another. And then, even as I struggled, it came to me to ponder this: under what circumstances would I be wearing a three-piece suit and need to clip a toenail? Anyone in his right mind would clip his toenails before getting into a three-piece suit; it does not come about that a man fully and formally dressed suddenly concludes that a toenail needs attention. Certainly not when he has gone out for the evening (which presumably is why the manufacturers think he needs it on his watch-chain); he does not turn up at this elegantly clad function of his and, as the toastmaster barks his name, suddenly decide it is time to rip his footwear off and roll about on the floor trying to get his feet up to his waistcoat.

Even if he has brought his plastic bag. I said I should come to this later, and I have; for the tiny leaflet shows a foot with a plastic bag over it. Inside the bag, there is also a hand. The hand is operating a Theta. It is a Useful Tip. "Placing a plastic bag over your foot will ensure clippings do not fly about the room."

Oh, come on! Do the makers really think that that would placate your hostess! If you tried it in ancient Greece, they'd have stuck a theta on your voting form so fast your feet wouldn't have touched the ground.

A Common Man's Guide to the Turf

Once, in the sweet lang syne, I had Turbary, Marl, Estover and Pannage. Not, as every Commoner knows, my firm of solicitors: firmer even than that, they were the law itself. In those days we owned a ramshackle New Forest go-down, which was gone down to at weekends so that we could plod about relishing pastoral things, among which nothing was more pastoral than Turbary, Marl, Estover and Pannage.

They were Commoners' Rights, which attached to New Forest property and enfranchised the lucky hut-holder to push a wheelbarrow out of his gate and bring it back again piled high with woodland. Turbary was the right to dig turf, Marl the right to dig clay, and Estover the right to gather fuel-wood. Pannage (aka Mast) was different, being the right to turn pigs out to root for acorns, and it remains a source of mortification to me that I was never able to exercise it, because I am a frugal man who has always hated the thought of acorns going to waste, and there is no other use for the acorn than putting it into a pig. But as we didn't own one – it was grim enough belting down the M3 every Friday night with a carload of moaningly deracinated infants determined not to know what was good for them, without having a pig on the back seat grunting about all the fun it was going to miss in London – my annual acorn catchment was infuriatingly left to rot.

But of Turbary, Marl and Estover I took full advantage. Happy as a pig in Pannage, I would spend each weekend trundling the forest fruits back to my premises, landscaping banks of clay, turfing them into rolling hummocks, and, when night fell upon my shredded ligaments, lying before a crackling log fire, for there is nothing more satisfying to the countryman than that rich smoky aroma produced when flying slivers of blazing faggot meet recently fitted carpet.

Yesterday, this all came plangently back. Yesterday was when I decided to remove a bed of old roses from my Cricklewood lawn because they were not old roses any more, they were old

160

sticks. I had given them one more year to produce something, but when the best their etiolated sap could squeeze out were a couple of pitiful excrescences which sprang into the world full-wizened and fell off the next day, I thought it kindest to put all of us out of our misery. This left me with a scar in the lawn four yards by three, and it seemed the most sensible course simply to turf it over.

It grew less sensible with every phone-call. I could find no garden centre prepared to deliver less than 100 square yards of the stuff, which, at £2.25 per sq yd, makes an old Commoner's scalp crinkle: once, I should merely have shouldered a shovel, arranged *Hi-ho, Hi-ho!* upon my lips and marched into the forest to get it. Upon which thought, a second smartly followed: was Hampstead Heath not common land? What was there to stop me nipping up the road and chiselling a mere 12 sq yds out of the available 4,000,000?

Everything. After an hour of being brusquely fobbed from department to department, since that is bound to be the way it is with something which has chosen to call itself the London Residuary Body, a pinch-voiced *kapo* finally had his day made by being able to tell me that the Heath had ceased to be common land in 1870 and had been redesignated a Metropolitan Open Space, which meant that any unauthorised person pulling even a weed up would render himself liable to public hanging, his relatives being forbidden to reclaim the body until the crows had had a good go. Still, I persisted; knowing how blind an eye the law often turns to Heath activities more nefarious even than contraband turf-cutting, I rang Hampstead nick and said, look, we are both men of the world, would anyone really mind if I took 12 yards of turf off the Heath? But since all I heard was the unmistakable noise of a copper dropping senseless to the lino, I quickly rang off before the call could be traced.

Well, you can take the boy out of the forest, but you can't take the forest out of the boy. Since it is a matter of brandy for the parson and turfage for the hack, I intend to be up there tonight with boot-lid raised and shovel swinging, and should any of the Heath's more typical nocturnal lawbreakers grow more than usually agitated in their busy undergrowth, my message to them is: Watch the wall, my darlings, while the Commoner runs by!

APRIL

Fish Out of Water

I have a pregnant goldfish. But do not write to congratulate me. Do not start knitting things.

Such kindnesses would be premature. I have passed this way before. Every April, I stroll through the back garden, green shoots below, plump buds above, to check for consonant burgeonings in the pond, and, sure enough, every year one of my two dozen fish is duly swollen. It is with egg. It is not always the same fish, but let us not get sidetracked into why this should be, because before we know it we shall find ourselves speculating as to what makes a fish attractive, what makes other fish fancy it one year but not the next, and what the complex social and sexual mores are which obtain in six cubic yards of Cricklewood water to ensure that only one female per annum ever, as my mother would have put it, falls. Having learned to tread warily in the semantics of modern feminism, I do not of course put it that way myself, I do not even know why my mother's generation put it that way, it seems a bit glum, but I don't intend to start rummaging through dictionaries, it's bad enough that my desk is piled high with ichthyological texts.

These being what you lug home from the library if you want little fish.

Because if you don't, you have no way of stopping what big fish want, which is little fish, too, but they want them somewhat differently: they want to eat them. For fish are paedophagic; worse yet, they do not gobble only other fish's offspring, they also gobble their own. Why they should have developed this repugnant habit is beyond me, nothing could be more literally counter-productive, but that is what fish do.

It is a source of unremitting annual distress to the caring pondholder. Every April, he is forced to wake from his pre-lapsarian dream. Once, I was God: I dug a hole to create a little world, I looked upon it and saw that it was good, I said "Be fruitful, and multiply," but I shrewdly rested after the fifth day, believing that if I stopped at fish, all would remain innocent. No one was going to offer fish an apple. I didn't know they didn't have to. I didn't know that fish came with built-in sin. I didn't know that when one became fruitful, the other 23 swam round it waiting for it to multiply so that they could all tuck in.

Well, this year I am putting a stop to it. You can do that if you're God, and have a library ticket. I have filleted everything from *You and Your Pond* to *You and Your Fish*, and, under their instruction, I have built a nursery. You might not recognise it as such, it does not have Womble wallpaper, it does not have a Mickey Mouse mobile, the uninformed would register it as a tin bath full of weeds and walk on, but a nursery is what it is. Somewhere in the weeds is the pregnant fish, poised to lay a million eggs, and as soon as she does this, I, as galvanised as the nursery itself, will be on her in a trice and, even as she begins to salivate, will place her on the other side of the loose muslin partition which bisects the bath, go to the pond, select a male, and pop him in beside her. He will then, I am told, begin hurling himself at the muslin, which will allow him to fertilise the eggs, but will not let him through to eat them; thus, after a bit, I shall have a million titchy fish on one side of the curtain, driving their disgusting parents into a gourmand, but impotent, frenzy. I shall then replace the adult fish in the pond.

166

Fine. But what happens next? The books do not say; I turn the page to find that, like some brusque midwife, they have washed their hands, remounted their Rudges, and pedalled away. Leaving me with a million infants, never mind what happens when I plop the parents back in the pond and 22 by-now-ravenous diners start shouting "Where's our bloody lunch?" All that the books say is that baby fish should not be placed in the pond until they are too large to be attacked. Have you any idea what a million fish too large to be attacked will look like? Forget the tin bath, I shall need the Serpentine.

I have thought long and hard about what I have started, and there would seem to be only one way to finish it. I shall ring up Macfisheries and tell them I am in a position to lay my hands on a reliable supply of whitebait. It would be a terrible waste to let all those little fish go uneaten.

Not Quite Correct

This morning, though the ensuing folderol demands total caution, I have no option but to proceed with total abandon. That is because I am assembling it from words. Were it possible to fashion it from Plasticine or strum it on the banjo, it might do less damage, but even then nothing is certain: these days, the risk of a racist crotchet is not lightly to be disregarded, nor can we be sure that young lives might not be ruined by passive modelling. Expose, say, an aquiline child to an insensitively sculpted conk, and who can be certain that he might not decide to spend the rest of his life with his head in a sack?

But words are the worst. Words are big trouble. They say things, but the things they say may, on occasion, be different from the things they say they say. And that, in these caring times, is totally unacceptable. Suppose, in the course of my imminent argument, I were to describe something as a black mark, a bald statement, a crippling liability, a dumb idea, a lame excuse, suppose I were to refer to yellow behaviour, blind panic, gay abandon, short shrift (all of which, indeed, clamour to be deployed), just think of the breadth of unintentional insult they would embrace!

All this started, quietly enough, with Alison Uttley. A day or so ago, I was sent a PEN survey on censorship in which, flipping through as one does, I noticed that the majority of publishers were now refusing to allow authors to use the word "pig" in children's books for fear of offending Muslims. A pity, I thought: this must mean that large numbers of British children were excluded from the reading community on the grounds that Sam Pig, despite his floppy hat, red waistcoat and impeccable manners, was unclean. He was not a little chap at all. He was crackling. He was lard. He was not, unfortunately, Sam Chicken. If he had been Sam Chicken, everybody could have read about him.

So, too, everybody could have read about Peter Chicken. I assume that Orthodox Jews do not want their children to read about Peter Rabbit, rabbits being, to them, as dietarily incorrect as pigs, but Peter Chicken would be all right. Just as, I suppose, it would be all right for Hindu children if a chicken jumped over the moon. You may conclude from this that children's fiction stands poised to become a trifle unvarious, there are a lot of unclean animals out there, we could be looking at *Chicken of Chicken Hall* and *Orlando the Marmalade Chicken*, but at least they wouldn't upset anyone.

For *Alice in Wonderland*, I hold out little hope, given that Alice follows a rabbit down a hole to meet a duchess who throws a baby about before turning into a pig; apart from all the ethnic unacceptability involved, it is clearly on the cards that Fergie, say, would sue on behalf of defamed single-parent aristocrats everywhere, a minority, I would remind you, whose

168

numbers grow less negligible by the hour. Mind you, she'd be on shaky ground, given her *Budgie* books; many poor children do not have helicopters, and if, as the PEN survey claims, authors are now discouraged even from mentioning big houses and grassy lawns on the grounds that grounds are what most children do not have, I doubt that her publishers would relish the publicity.

They would prefer to be out commissioning *The Squat at Pooh Corner* or *Five Go Into Care*, since such would be more, where's that survey again, "relevant" than ballet lessons, gymkhanas, midnight feasts in dorms, or the "unacceptably supernatural" doings of witches, goblins and the rest. And, of course, as each manuscript arrived, a crack editorial *Waffenkommando* would pounce, charged with the excision of any word deemed capable of a construction which might somehow disturb someone, somewhere. Which, of all the insanities that censorship invites, is quite the maddest of all; to divide or marginalise kids by race, class, background, belief, or whatever else, is appalling enough, to limit their opportunity either to experience a real world which is not theirs or to exercise an imagination which allows them to transcend both is equally monstrous, but to intervene between them and the limitless possibilities of language is ... well, words fail me.

Just Digging Your Own Grave

O
f all the myriad wonders on which Cricklewood's transglobal renown is deservedly founded, there is perhaps none worthier than her Institute for Social Inventions. Housed at 20 Hever Road NW2, the ISI is committed to nothing less than the perpetual search to improve man's lot upon this hapless planet by spotting the potential of stuff anyone might find in the average dustbin and, with a tin-tack here and a reef-knot there, deploying it to the benefit of less fortunate humankind. No challenge great or small, from, say, building a battered husbands' refuge out of old cotton-reels, to boiling down unwanted rabbit-skulls into a handy fixative guaranteed to stop Third World dentures from rattling in even the stiffest nor'easter, remains unrisen to.

Above all, in an era distinguished for the manufacture of rubbish both physical and spiritual, the Institute offers the concomitant chance of bipolar redemption, since anyone prepared to take a gutterful of contemporary jetsam and selflessly spend his day recycling it into some boon for the needy will soon feel his soul soar above the tacky bonds of earth. There is nothing like spray-painting an assortment of Big Mac cartons and Carlsberg cans and stringing them above an orphan's cot to set a man's feet on the path to beatification.

Mind you, you have to be a dab hand with gum and hammer. For some time now, the Institute has been sending me its newsletter, and I have to report that my ratio of execution to inspiration is disappointingly low. Much as I'd love to take a dozen Madonna albums and melt them into a dinner service fit to grace any Oxfam window, or separate from their scrapped camshaft the cams crying out to be converted into sturdy door-knockers so hard-of-hearing OAPs would not miss their wheeled meals, these and many another altruistic cobble have proved beyond my talent.

Which is why I view the upcoming Natural Death Dinner with some unease. On September 27, the Institute is convening what their latest bumf describes as a gourmet meal with wine for £12, a bargain I should normally snap up, were it not for the post-prandial topic, a discussion on "DIY Funerals" in preparation for which the Institute has circulated us with a digest of potential themes, viz:

Flatpack coffin: Richard Hoskin Workshops offer a flatpack coffin from £35 plus delivery, made of MDF, ply or veneer.

Making our own coffins: Barbara Huelin writes: My husband has recently finished building our coffins, in blockboard, at a cost of £50 each (not including our time). They are painted green and have nautical-looking rope handles. We have booked a double-decker site in the local council cemetery for £100, to which family and friends will bear us.

Fruit tree planted over body: Often, in the back country of Montana, a hole will be dug and the body in a plain pine coffin will be lowered in. Instead of a tombstone, a fruit tree is planted over the body. In the years to follow, eating the fruit will be like partaking in the loved one.

Um. While I applaud all this, and certainly don't wish my corpse to run up a huge post-mortal bill for having its golden casket trotted to its bespoke Richard Rogers mausoleum by six St Leger winners, I nevertheless spot a major snag in the Institute's cheapo alternative: given a lifetime's toolbox experience, can my deathtime's one be any better? Just as I have unpacked many a flatpacked thing and screwed it three-dimensional only to have it immediately fall flat again, so I have ruined more blockboard than most people have had gourmet dinners. As for nautical-looking rope handles, mine would not look nautical long: I have watched too many rowboats drift away from their bollards to have much confidence that, as family and friends bore me to my plot, my handles would not unravel, leaving my wonky ill-nailed blockboard flanks to drop, dismantle, and render their contents an embarrassment to all.

And when it comes to planting a fruit tree over me, once family and friends have scooped me back into the wheelbarrow, there is no question but that, on my past horticultural record, the

item I have pre-mortally ordered from the garden centre will
turn out to have scab, mildew, leaf-curl, canker, and sawflies; if,
indeed, it is not already deader than I am.

You wouldn't want to eat anything growing on it. Unless, that
is, you were so Green you hated the idea of a double-decker plot
going to waste.

Guess What's Bugging Me

Since Franklin D. Roosevelt neglected to observe that the
only thing we have to worry about is worry itself, you can
tell that he did not do his own unpacking. It is one of the
great perks of high office: you get off the plane, and the next
time you see your bits and bobs they are all stashed neatly away,
shoes here, shirts there, soiled stuff in the laundry-basket, and
anything crawling out of the suitcase dealt with by a civil
servant. And if there is any worrying about it to be done, it is
the civil servant who lies awake staring at the ceiling.

Lacking, however, a *chef de ménage*, I returned from France
yesterday to do the stuff with the shoes and shirts myself; and it
all went well enough until the suitcase was empty, at which
point it stopped going well because the suitcase was not empty
at all. I discovered this when, having finished stashing, I went to
shut it. There was a thing crawling out of it. The thing so far
had only a couple of legs over the edge, but after a bit it had a
lot of legs over the edge, plus a fair number of wings and
antennae, and after that it crawled down the outside of the
suitcase and began examining the carpet. The carpet threw it.
You could tell that from the antennae. The thing was worried.

It was not alone.

In the old days, of course, before we were all whole-earth, lead-free, foxiphile, free-range, fur-shunning, caring organic New Men, I should not have worried at all. If a thing which had crawled into my suitcase in France had crawled out of it again in England, I should have stepped on it. My sole concern would have been, quite literally, that: for it used to be a tricky and unsavoury business, scraping insect detritus off your shoe. You had to hop somewhere that had a knife and a bin and a tap.

Entomological rectitude, however, has changed all that; we no longer step on things lightly, we worry about them, and, even worse, we worry about worrying about them, because we lack the wherewithal to know exactly what it is we ought to be worrying about.

Take yesterday's thing. It was roughly an inch long, with burnished-copper wings folded neatly behind a round, slightly horned head, the whole borne about on six hairy little legs. To all intents and purposes, a beetle, whatever the intents and purposes of beetles are, and finely wrought: had you seen it on a woman's lapel, you would have commended her taste, unless she happened to be screaming at you to get it off.

Now, while I have observed millions of these items scuttling around the Mediterranean, I have never observed one in Cricklewood. Thus the worries began: if I scooped it caringly off the carpet and liberated it into the garden, would it briefly take account of the fact that it was several degrees colder here than in Provence, and then pop its six little clogs? And if it did survive the temperature, would it find nourishment to its liking, or slowly starve? And if it did adapt itself to English tucker, would it find a mate, or mope around in celibate gloom until it died, alone and unfulfilled? And if it did find some domestic bug susceptible to its Gallic charm, would that be any better? Might my uninformed pandering not result in some horrible franglais hybrid, invulnerable to natural enemy or pesticide, which would soon, in its unstoppable billions, proceed to munch our entire landscape? I may not understand much about chaos theory, but any fool knows that Pandora's box is full of horseshoe-nails.

What alternative, then? Pop it in a matchbox and repatriate it, contrary to God knows what lurking Maastricht footnote? Worse, have it expire en route, and find myself up before the Hague beak on a hydra-headed charge of causing unnecessary suffering to an illegal export deprived of political asylum and, furthermore, contravening Europostal regulations regarding the cross-Channel mailing of meat possibly infected with Mad Insect Disease?

Twenty-four hours on, the thing is in a jar in the kitchen, with a lot of English grass. It is impossible to tell whether it has eaten any of it, though it seems happy enough, but neither of us is any closer to a solution. And yes, I did consider dialling the London Zoo, but the caring finger froze after three digits. They have enough worries of their own.

The Night They Bombed Caruso

I have been thinking about income tax. Moreover, I have come to a conclusion; my conclusion is that if it hadn't been for income tax, a zeppelin would have got Caruso.

Now, I have never been a fan of linear history. I find the sequential ordering of the past to be a lifeless business. This happened, then that, and after that, this. Discuss. It cannot hold a candle (which is, after all, history's brief) to the collateral approach. Tell me that even as George Washington was being inaugurated, William Blake was galloping down to the printers with *Songs of Innocence*, only to be stopped at Ludgate Hill by a man enquiring whether he had heard what was going on outside the Bastille, and 1789 begins to breathe for me.

And so to Cricklewood, for a tale of two nannies.

A few days ago, a reader sent me an obituary from *The Independent* which told the remarkable story of Nesta Cox, English nanny to a noble French family who, with her, worked for the Resistance. Her latter heroism, however, was not my correspondent's purpose in writing; the sentence underlined for my attention was: "After training, she started work at the age of 15 during the First World War and was bombed from a zeppelin, to no effect, while looking after children in Cricklewood."

I do not need to be told such things twice: we in the brick business know straw when we see it. Hitherto unaware that the Kaiser had earmarked Cricklewood as the fulcrum of his ambition, I was off to the archives in a trice; and by yesterday, I found myself in possession of a jigsaw so much more complete than the picture on the original box that the gooseflesh sprang. Allow me to conflate my cullings.

It is a moonlit February night in 1915, and to the north of Dortmund, Zeppelin LR17 rises slowly to 12,000 feet, and turns on a westward heading. Though Hendon's RAF Museum records are sadly not as explicit on this point as on others, nothing will shake my belief that it is a member of the famed Krickelwald Escadrille, hand-picked by Wilhelm II to strike at the heart of Allied morale by taking out England's loveliest village. To this end, LR17 releases, a little after 10 p.m., a stick of 50kg bombs over Shoot-Up Hill, demolishing two Edwardian villas and damaging five more, including the one in which Nanny Cox is reading her little charges to sleep.

Glancing up from *Peter Pan* with no more than the reproving tut her legendary fortitude allows – I admit to a little glossing here, the contemporary *Kilburn Times* having been subject to War Office censorship – Nanny Cox neither knows nor cares that the empty house two doors away has been flattened.

I know, though. I also know who wasn't in it.

On April 25, 1914, Enrico Caruso arrived from New York and went to Clarendon Court, Maida Vale, where he owned a flat containing his son and Nanny Saer. History does not record what Nanny Saer was reading aloud from, either, but you can be sure she stopped when her boss burst in, because Enrico was in a rage, and when Enrico shouted, windows shattered. What had upset him was that the Inland Revenue had judged that his flat made him an English resident, and subject to income tax. So he sold the flat, and moved a mile up the Edgware Road to a house in Shoot-Up Hill owned by Nanny Saer's parents, where the Caruso family could stay without giving Herbert Asquith sixpence in the pound.

But the Inland Revenue were not so easily cheated. They continued to hound Enrico until, in September 1914, the family moved out for good. Now, can you guess where that house was two doors away from? I cannot, of course, say with absolute certainty that, five months later, Caruso would have been gargling his tubes when LR17 hove to overhead, but does even an outside chance not make the neck-hairs bristle?

Do you know Symptosis? She is the tenth Muse, and her portfolio is coincidence. She can be a remarkable help to hacks.

Danger: Heavy Plant Crossing

Though I acknowledge the risk that it may make you bury your face in your pinny and shriek uncontrollably until help arrives, let me call today's wittering a manifesto. I swear I should not do so were there a more appropriate word, but since manifesto derives from *manus* (hand) and *festus* (struck), there is not. Take my word for it. A hand has struck, and something must be done about it if civilisation is not to sink irrecoverably into an abyss so beyond our capacity to imagine that even Dante wouldn't know where to start.

On Monday night, we returned from a weekend away with no more than a householder's normal trepidation, i.e. check all chimneys for sudden absence, turn key in front door, listen for reassuring bleep of undisturbed alarm but keep ear cocked for alien footfall, drip, or crackle, flare nostril for gas, then proceed up stairs and . . . and stop halfway.

Something was wrong. But its wrongness was not susceptible to the available organs, it was one of those wrongnesses that well up from vague awareness; an unease. I did not know what it was until I came downstairs again and went to collect the suitcase I had left on the step while I opened the door. The suitcase should have been beside something which should have been beside the step. A hydrangea. It had been there for twenty years. It was not there any more. What was there was a large hole. There was just enough light from the hall to see, at the bottom of the hole, a few pitiful white squiggles, snapped off where they still grappled the earth in testament to the fight without which a plucky hydrangea will not give up. A stranger would call them roots. I would call them toes.

For some shrubs you get close to. Some shrubs are family. When we moved into the house in 1972, people came with pot plants; two were hydrangeas, and after the people had gone away again, we planted the infant shrublets either side of the front door, whereafter they were cherished, mulched, fed, and bought regular large ones of aluminium sulphate to keep them blue. They grew, they throve, and they complemented one another bloom for bloom. Now one of them has nothing to complement. I looked at the house this morning, and it was as if it had one ear. Some bastard stole up in the night and stole away again, and what he has stolen is more than a shrub, he has stolen twenty years.

And he has done even more than that, he has left me at several losses. What kind of bastard can this be? He is clearly not a horticultural bastard, because the plant had already begun to leaf up; it is too late to transplant it, and the bastard will have to shift it quickly if his motive was profit, because if he does not shift it quickly he will be going door to door with a corpse. As you might guess, I have mixed feelings on this: while for the plant's sake I want it to live, for the bastard's sake I want it to die.

But this is only the tip of the confusion he has wrought. Perhaps he was not a professional bastard at all but a neighbourhood amateur, bent on improving his tract at the expense of mine. If so, am I to trudge Cricklewood's verdant lanes, looking for something beloved and wilting so that I can take the bastard by the throat? But, if further so, how will I know if the hydrangea is mine and not a mere victim of some brown-fingered nerd? You cannot take people by the throat on such slim evidence, they will croak for the Old Bill even as you throttle.

Then there is the question of what to put in the hole. You cannot buy a hydrangea as large as the one that went, unless you know a bastard, in which case it will be on its last legs anyhow, so am I to plant a titchy one and wait another 20 years for a matched pair? And, to reach the manifesto part of this manifesto, where were my neighbours, the police, the three political parties, when all that digging was going on? In other words, What Is To Be Done? We have grown used to fortifying our houses, so are we now, as things fall even further apart, to start fortifying our gardens, too? Hide mantraps in the aubretia, wire up each rosebush to the local nick, install a Dobermann in the rockery?

In short, if even hydrangeas are not safe in their beds, is any of us?

MAY

Pole Position

I don't know how early you rose this morning to tug the newspaper through your flap, but I do know that it wasn't nearly early enough to catch the Magdalen College choristers in their cots. They were long gone. They had risen even before the dawn itself had got around to it, they had gurgled one last gargle to bring their little glottises to perfect pitch, they had shimmied into their scarlet cassocks, and they had set off on the long climb to the top of Magdalen Tower to form serried ranks and, on the peal of 6 a.m., beat the skylarks at their own aubadal game.

So that by the time you read this, they will almost certainly have abseiled down again, having put yet another *Te Deum Patrem Colimus* triumphantly behind them, just as their trilling forebears had done every May Day morning since the one in 1773 when they sang it for the first time, in place of the far longer oratorio they had been singing for the umpteen years before that. Because, as you may recall, it was coming down cats and dogs on May 1 1773, and the bedraggled songsters were not only so late in getting to the tower, but also so

181

knackered at being compelled to scale it at the double, that time and breathlessness required them to substitute for their traditional concert repertoire that concise chunk of the college grace which they subsequently decided to stick with, for there is nothing like a public cock-up to get an English tradition off the ground; that is why we have the Light Brigade to thank for cardigans and matching woolly hats.

Why do the choristers do this? Does May-singing share the ritualistic folderol of May-poling, May-birching, May-garlanding, May-staving, May-queening, or any other of the coyly indelicate celebrations that combine soft floral circlets and long stiff staffs in order to remind us what our fancy is seasonally expected lightly to turn to? Well, yes, it does rather (otherwise Morris dancers would not, at the close of the singing, hurtle through Oxford in that frenzy of crypto-eroticism for the most part lost on the goggling tourist), and in a very peculiar way, too. Because the traditional means of arriving at the bottom of Magdalen Tower in order best to appreciate what is happening at the top has always been the punt: and one, what's more, in which a young man and a young woman have spent the previous night ostensibly in mystic union with riparian sprites, but in fact, given average luck, going at it like staffs and garlands.

Let us now turn to one of Oxford's even more significant contributions to the culture, the *OED*, where we find a *double entendre* so delightfully right for the present purposes that it might very well bring us to the point. "Punt: a kind of Gallic transport." *A kind of Gallic transport*! Could there be a definition more consonant with the lexicographer's decorous nib than this attempt to convey with propriety the improper associations of a word his professional duty requires him to address? We know what Gallic transport is all right, it is ooh-la-la, it is the pleasure, and the gift, of mademoiselles from Armentières, it is, in short, what happens to people at that moment when the earth moves for them, which it noticeably tends to in a punt, as vernal sunlight dapples their tingling skin, and bluebirds collide ecstatically above them, and coupling toads plash in a lusty sub-plot on the bank, acknowledging the spring with every hormone in their warty bodies.

Et in Arcadia ego, provided you can say that without getting buried first. I, too, have lain willow-hidden in the gnatty Oxford gloaming and scattered Cherwell minnows with cold bangers jettisoned, half-finished, because other appetites suddenly pressed; I, too, have stood shivering as May crept in, up to my numb waist in sunken punts among the bobbing bras and bottles, while boy sopranos smugly asserted their innocence two hundred feet above. Nor, since you ask, was mine an undab hand at the pole itself; it had to be, then, because those not to the manner born felt that they owed that much to those who had offered them the chance of the manner learnt: if you were a Fifties grammar-school boy, you took your counter-jumping seriously, and there was nothing like a punt-pole to help you vault it, you could quit the social class which sat pulling itself backwards with two bits of wood and paying for it with half-a-crown, to join the social class which stood pushing itself forwards with one bit of wood and paying for it on account.

Given which, and also the nauseating nostalgia you will already have picked up at every turn of this ramble, it suddenly came upon me, when I was invited to help *The Times* celebrate May Day, to roll down the arches of the years until I came to the one marked Magdalen Bridge and see how much water had, interim, rolled under it, I took it in mind, that is, to convene a little party of my *jeunesse dorée* contemporaries, hire a punt for the night of April 30 and, having frittered the small hours away in booze and soppy reminiscence, pole it towards the dawn chorus.

So am I, then, as you merely read this, living it? Wait.

Since I did not wish to appear even more of a prat than the entire enterprise suggested, I thought it no bad plan to go up to Oxford last Sunday, solicit a punt at Magdalen Bridge, and get my hand in, or, rather, up and down: which would have, furthermore, the benefit of providing *The Times* with a photograph to accompany the commissioned text. So I duly settled an unsettled paparazzo at one end, erected myself shakily at the other, and shoved off. And surprisingly, the hands quickly rediscovered their cunning and the sensitivity to silt and eddy returned, so that by the time I slid bumplessly back alongside the punt-landing, I was confident in my booking of an overnight punt, cash up front for the coming May Morning eve. The puntmaster, however, shook his head.

"Night-punting's been banned," he said.

"*Banned?*" I cried. "Why?"

"People got drunk," he said.

"But they always got drunk."

"They got up to, you know."

"But they always got up to it."

"They fell in."

"But they always fell in."

"The punts went walkabout, or sank."

"But they always went walkabout, or sank."

He needed a clincher. You could tell.

"Jeremy Irons," he said, "used to keep a private punt here, a very nice punt, cost a fortune, folding canopy, full recliners, you could live on that punt, anyway, one night it was nicked, what do you think of that, Jeremy Irons's punt nicked?"

"Quite appalling." I said. "The man won an Oscar."

"There you are then," said the puntmaster.

Here I am, then. In bed in Cricklewood, on May Morning. I shall dress in a bit, go down to my pond, see if the frogs are up to anything festive, have a glass of Bollinger, wink an eye at the woman next door. I may even take my ukulele. It won't be the same, of course, but these days, what is?

Birds' Nest Soup

You will say that I have chosen a pretty dumb time to get into the property business. Things, you will smugly parrot off your monitory telly, can go down as well as up. But it is precisely because things can go down as well as up that I have got into the property business.

There was a gale last night. That is why the thing went down. I knew it had gone down as soon as I crept into the loft to hack this morning, because bang opposite my attic window, at the far end of the garden, there is a bare ruin'd choir where late the sweet birds sang, and this morning it was a bit more ruin'd than it had been yesterday: the thing the sweet birds had built to have something to sing in, possibly indeed to sing about, had gone down. A huge nest which had hitherto nestled in an upper fork of my acacia tree was now on the lawn beneath. A number of birds, moreover, were ambling about looking at it: wood-pigeons, blackbirds, sparrows, the odd magpie. Nothing special: this is Cricklewood. There hasn't been a toucan all year.

I could not of course, from that distance, tell what these birds were thinking. Even a major ornithologist would be hard-pushed, at 50 feet, to distinguish between avian grief, say, and curiosity, surprise and irritation. But I could see they were interested. A fallen nest was clearly a big event. It was something to chirp home about. So I went down for a shufti of my own. The crowd of birds dispersed, but only to observe me from fence and tree and sundial; they wanted to know what a man would do with a nest. Time would prove that they were not alone.

It was a large nest, some two feet across, and surprisingly heavy. What we in the property business would describe as a substantial detached family residence, constructed from traditional materials and finished to a high standard to suit the most discriminating taste, the exterior in sturdy latticed twig, the interior furnished with fine moss, grass and mud, and the whole held together by best spit (at least, that is what I have long understood birds' nests to be held together with; it is what has always, when the Chinese soup menu is offered, made me opt for won ton).

The nest between my hands was, in short, an impressive artefact. Much time, talent, and effort had patently gone into it; it was, furthermore, resonant with the sentimental input common to all domestic premises – a mutually besotted young couple had built it with their own beaks, raised their offspring in it, and, when love finally lost its battle with duty, booted them from its rim, to watch, weeping as only birds can, while the kids fluttered ineptly off to new lives of their own. You could not just bung a thing like that on the compost heap. Especially as it seemed in pristine nick. This was a quality nest: might it not still be a des. res. to suit lge. fmly.?

I came inside again and rang the RSPB. Oh yes, said Mr Barton, nests were indeed re-used, often year after year, getting even bigger and better in the process; and, what was more, some birds sought to return to re-use their own nests, provided they hadn't been taken over by birds of prey. He also, bless him, faxed me several pages of information to help me identify the property-owner in question, since different birds build different sorts of nest in different trees at different heights.

This, you will already have guessed, was far less help to me than the helpful Mr Barton intended; it left me with options, each of which was more unfathomable than the last. I could, for example, put the nest back in the acacia, but I could not put it back where it was before, because they are whippy things, acacias, you do not want to climb above a certain height. I should have to wedge it in a lower fork. If I wanted to relocate the nest at its former height, I could do it only in the pear tree. Alternatively, if I preferred to stay out of traction, I could simply shove it, shoulder height, in a hedge. But since I could not only not put it where it was before but could not even identify which bird had built it, all these options boded future trouble: the returning birds would say hallo, what is our home doing down here/over there, we are woodpigeons, what is it doing at blackbird height, why is it in a hedge etc, whereupon they would have a look inside and find either that blackbirds had

186

indeed moved in, or that a bird of prey had beaten all of them to it, and what would the woodpigeons, if that's what they were, could be magpies, do then? They are not built to have a go at a condor, they would probably end up fighting among themselves, he shrieking this is the wrong garden altogether, I told you we should have turned left at Wembley, she crying none of this would have happened if you'd built a new nest, I never liked the old one anyhow, all them weeds . . .

They might well, as a result, split up. Destined eggs would not get laid. Worse, who knew, one woodpigeon might resign itself to living on alone at magpie height and end up mating out with some undiscriminating jay. Chaos theory could reign. As the result of my well-meaning intervention, pigeons might one day mutate into amphibious gastropods and hairy sparrows spin their webs in chimney corners. Johnny evolution is an unpredictable cove, look at the duck-billed platypus, it might well have started out as a variety of chaffinch before some Neanderthal columnist with more ecophilia than sense began splashing irresponsibly around in Time's ever-rolling stream.

It is gloaming as I write, and the nest is still on the lawn where I left it. From time to time, various birds approach for a bit of a poke about, as if wondering what it will fetch in today's depressed market or just, perhaps, looking for decor tips, but as for me, I remain fraught with indecision. There is, mind, an alternative course of action which is gradually coming to commend itself as both recyclingly correct and at the same time reasonably free of interventionist risk: if I attached three bits of string to it, I should have an organic hanging-basket that any conservationist would be proud to dangle.

Not Cricket

Could spell trouble, this one. We may well be talking drumhead court martial here, your correspondent frog-marched between two burly groundstaff into the Long Room, where, on the committee table, the cricket bat lies with its handle pointed away from him to announce that there is nought for it but to chew the lip as his tie is snipped off at the knot and his Gent's Premier Panama is formally trodden on.

And it will be scant consolation to him to reflect that at least it wasn't a Gent's Superior Panama: the fact that only £19.95 has gone up the spout instead of £35 will hardly compensate for the grim knowledge that he has just been dishonourably discharged from the MCC.

But should this happen, justice will have grossly miscarried, and if I am forced by society's uninformed disgust to end up cleaning out the latrines of Fort Zinderneuf, I shall bear my exile without shame. For what I write is written not from disloyalty but from love, and written furthermore on this Tuesday, knowing that that very love will ensure my presence at Lord's tomorrow, among my judges: were they to glance up from the newspaper trembling furiously between their hands and flecked with the pork-pie shards their rage has coughed upon this column (for it is the lunch interval), they might very well spot me sitting a mere stump-shy away. I shall even make it easier for them, because my convictions give me courage: I am the one without the MCC blazer, cufflinks, umbrella, braces, buttons or cushion, and should you wish further proof of my identity, ask, while time remains before England and Pakistan re-emerge, to have a shufti at my wallet or my key-ring; neither, you will find, sports the club monogram.

For some time now, the annual MCC sales catalogue of distinguishing accoutrements has been growing ever fatter. Once, a member would buy a tie, possibly a hatband for a straw he already had, and be content to leave it at that. Well, not entirely at that: he would have to flick a blob or two of soup

188

onto the tie and spit on the hatband to simulate sweat so none would think him a novice, but that was about it. Not only was he not offered, as he is in the 1993 list, all the insigniated items mentioned above, nor was he beguiled with a set of six MCC coasters to match his set of six MCC platter mats, nor an MCC handpainted wall-shield to complement his MCC car-badge. Nor, I submit, would he have wanted them: for while it is quite acceptable to declare your pride at belonging to the world's greatest club by tying a ribbon around your neck for Lord's, who with any gill of humankindness would seek constantly to remind the hapless unelected of their exclusion by inviting them round to sit on an MCC cushion beneath an MCC wall-shield while he, provocatively blazered, bow-tied, braced and cuff-linked, slipped an emblazoned coaster beneath their gin prior to feeding them off an MCC platter until it was time to escort them, beneath his MCC umbrella, to the pitifully badgeless car parked beside his own?

No good banging on, you say, this is the age of the logo, live and let live, but it is not as simple as that: while the badge is about membership, the logo is about marketing, and if I want, as I do, the MCC to prosper, how can I stand idly by? I ought not only to buy all these natty baubles for myself and become their living advertisement (despite the risk of wags coming up to me on the street and asking for two tickets for *The Boy Friend*), I ought constantly to be advancing brilliant new suggestions to the secretary: what about MCC caftans, eggcups, deckchairs, condoms? I ought to be pressing urgently for the inclusion of women in the membership, given the limitless marketing extension this would represent, I ought to be scouring the landscape for potential MCC-DIY hypermarket sites where members could purchase the paints and wallpapers and tiles to turn their homes into the red-and-gold-striped declaration of their status.

But I cannot. The Gent's Premier Panama was as far as I could bring myself to go, and even that I don't intend to put on tomorrow until I'm halfway down St John's Wood Road. True, I shall be taking it out of a plastic bag marked Waitrose, but I don't mind carrying that. You don't look flash with a Waitrose logo. Anyone can join.

Putting on the Dog

I am building a dog. It's coming along quite nicely, all things considered, even if some things unconsidered have caused the odd glitch; for example, you'd think you could find a set of bent hocks prefitted with round tight toes, but you can't. While, according to Cruft's, there are all kinds of feet to be found attached to bent hocks, including arched oval, hare-toed, and even the somewhat recherché knuckled-up, round tight toes do not come as standard. They have to be ordered separately.

As a consequence of this, my dog does not yet have legs. It has a finely chiselled head, it has broad chops and well-sprung ribs, it has well-angulated hindquarters and a tail set high at the insertion, but it has no legs. This is a serious shortcoming given that the dog's main duties will be to accompany me on long nocturnal walks and fetch things lost about the house, e.g., fags, library tickets, car keys, and so on. Leglessness will thus be something of a handicap. I do not wish to amble the night pulling my dog behind me on a little trolley, a prey to every cat and joker, nor, pressed for a smoke or library book, do I want to hang about all day while my dog rolls slowly towards them.

I may have to compromise on the legs; take whatever feet they come with. I fancied tight round toes as being (a) likely to leave smaller footprints on the carpet after wet walks, and (b) safer from harm at crowded parties when a careless brogue could mean major veterinary bills and – if the dog demonstrates any spirit – major lawsuits, but you can't have everything.

Ears have been a headache, too. I had been rather keen on lobular as being better for reflective fondling (mine, not the dog's), but they do not go with the chiselled head, and as the head is non-negotiable, we both seem to be stuck with ears erect and triangular, i.e. dust traps.

When did all this start? On the morning after my Friday piece about taking a midnight walk. I received a letter from a reader who said he was astonished to find no mention of my dog, for he'd been sure I was a dog owner; and as he warmed hysterically to his theme, I divined that he saw man as having so great a duty to dogs that to stroll alone was a criminal waste of walking. So much so that if, as walker, I didn't have a dog, then I ought to buy one.

I thought for a bit. Working at home as I do, it would be agreeable to have a dog. There would be two of us to stare out of the window. But which breed? I rang a friend whose clothes are always covered in hair, and he said you need Erich Tylinek's *The Dog*, borrow it, it'll answer all your questions. What it did, of course, was question all my answers.

For example, I had already reached the point of choosing between an Irish Terrier and an Afghan, which I have always liked, but the book said the former was noted for its readiness to fight, while the latter was aloof and obstinate. So both were out, since I had no wish to while away the Cricklewood nights either prising my best friend's jaws from anything that moved or fondling the ears of a pig-headed snob. But if not these, what? The Karelian Bear-Dog, perhaps? "Bred expressly for big-game hunting", it would be just the thing to stun the strolling chic – yes, I'd say, we're off to bag a few rhino as soon as the weather perks up – but "it shuns domesticity". Lost keys would leave it cold. The Bloodhound, then? It will find anything, but "relishes several days' tracking". I would have to leave my glasses in Swindon, just to get it to accept the job. The Bergamaschi? "Gentle and modest" I warmed to, but "an ever-eager herddog"? You would not be able to take your eyes off it for a second. The garden would fill with waifs and milkmen.

All Sunday, I pored and annotated. I made Xeroxes, cut them up into canine components, mixed and matched. Did you know that there was no such thing as the perfect pooch? Until yesterday; yesterday, I arrived at my ideal identidog, tough but friendly, loyal but independent, keen on short walks, cheap food, fetching and carrying, and great to look at; at least, from the shoulder up. It is a Pyrenean Cockerpointing Setter-haired Sheephound, and as soon as I decide on a suitable set of legs, I shall ring Harrod's. I'm told they can track down anything.

Parting Shots

On the day you die, what do you want people to say about you? Well, yes, of course, you want them to say, "My God, 108, what a great innings!", but what do you want them to say next? How do you wish to be remembered? For your achievements? For your character? Or for some daft individuating feature, be it never so tiny, which, whenever your name is posthumously mentioned, instantly rings a bell and throws up an image, much in the manner of an ancient cash-register?

The odds, I have to tell you, are on the latter; history will see to that. Clio is a mischievous little operator, and can never resist fixing it so that if, say, you burned cakes, fled up an oak tree, required Hardy to kiss you or Bognor to be buggered, such minutiae will popularly supersede anything else. Which is why my heart goes out, today, not only to the late Sir Ian Jacob, but to me.

Yesterday, the *Daily Telegraph* ran an obituary of Sir Ian, into whose 93 years so many enterprises of great pith and moment had been packed – intellectual powerhouse of

192

Churchill's wartime cabinet, DG of the BBC, subsequent chairman, trustee, director of almost everything else – that, as I read, I found myself wondering what immemorial clincher the obituarist would pick to leave us with in summing up so teeming a public life. It was this: "In India, he shot big game, narrowly failing to bag a tiger." I read this several times; I could not decode it. The obituarist had chosen not only to sign off a life of almost unprecedented achievement with the one thing unachieved, but also to offer us an image which I, for one, will henceforth find ineradicable. Whenever Sir Ian's name is uttered, I shall see only the bespectacled and balding figure in the *Telegraph* mugshot, ineptly emptying his Remington from the top of an elephant, while something striped lopes gratefully away.

Which, mind, is still only a fragment of the picture. What does his chronicler mean by "narrowly failing"? Is that a good thing, or a bad? I mean, was it a tricky shot, e.g., a cheap gun, a nervous elephant, a titchy tiger, or did Sir Ian, perhaps, broadly succeed in bagging something else in error, a bearer, a nawab, a, worst of all, cow? We may never know, but I think some of us may think of little else for some considerable time.

I shall, because, as I hinted, this comes very close to home. At 54, I have reached half my allotted span, and not unnaturally begun to wonder what a bereft world may one day make of me. Now, it so happens that in 1966, my wife and I were charged by the Ford Motor Company with taking their very first Transit on a proving run through the northern Sahara, and because there were just the two of us, and (having read *Beau Geste*), I knew the desert to be an inimical spot, I persuaded Rochester Row to issue me with a firearms certificate and Cogswell & Harrison to sell me a Walther 9mm automatic, so that should a horde of armed Touaregs suddenly descend upon us, I should be able to spring from my vehicle, draw my pistol, and give it to them as a present.

They never materialised; two months later, as we drove through the outskirts of Cairo, the gun was still under my seat. At which point, a dog suddenly somersaulted above the car in front and rolled into the gutter; the driver did not stop, but we did, and got out, and the dog was in as bad shape as a dog can get, and my wife said, "Shoot it."

I don't know why it should be so hard to put a dog out of its misery, all I know is that it took a full clip, by which time most of suburban Cairo was on the street yelling, and since there was no way of proving we had acted not from malice but from pity (it was the tenth anniversary of Suez, and were anyone to take it into his head that the British were celebrating this with a revenge mission targeted on household pets, we should soon be in worse nick than the dog), we leapt smartly back aboard and drove to the nearest police station to explain, a matter involving several hundred forms and the British vice-consul.

They do not keep things to themselves, diplomats: when, a week later, we dropped into the Damascus embassy, our man said, "Oh yes, you're that silly arse who shot a dog in Egypt." Which is why I put it on the record now. It might stop someone else dragging it up in 54 years' time.

Stands Cricklewood Where it Did?

Sunday was a very big day for Cricklewood. Sunday was the day Cricklewood got very big. To understand why, we must go back 21 years to the day I bought a house in Hampstead. I had always wanted a house in Hampstead, it would match my painstakingly battered typewriter, it would match my fastidiously wrinkled corduroys, it would match my *amour propre* and my aspirations, it would, in short, set me up a treat for the literary life. More yet than that, Hampstead's osmotic air would actually power that life: sucked into the carburettor, it would produce so rich a mixture with the blood as to ensure a permanent heyday of creativity, I should be able to knock out stuff like that till the cows came home. Keats had lived in Hampstead, Leigh Hunt, Wilkie Collins, Wells, Lytton Strachey, Bennett, Galsworthy, Lawrence, Katherine Mansfield, Stephen Spender, J.B. Priestley, three sorts of du Maurier ... clearly, Hampstead was the literary equivalent of Carlsbad or Lourdes, a couple of lungfuls of Heath oxygen, a quick dunk in the Well Road slipper baths, and writer's block would be cured for ever, you would be able to take up your Olivetti and walk, the stuff would come rattling effortlessly out of it at 100 wpm, and every word a little gem. Added to which, at the close of each day's imperishable chapter, you would be off to any one of a dozen gamey boozers to chew the literary fat over a pint of absinthe with the best and the brightest, no, no, my shout, Kingsley, room for another pork scratching, Miss Drabble?

So I went into this estate agent's in Heath Street and told him I was looking for a house in Hampstead, and he pulled out a lot of brochures, and I peered at the asking prices, and after the red mist had ebbed, it struck me that Keats had clearly had a bob or two, there must have been real money in odes, once, but I did not remark on this to the agent, because there was little about him to bespeak a fan of the anapaest, I merely told him how much the Halifax reckoned I was good for, so he opened a different drawer, and we set off in his Vauxhall, and I said somewhere up near Whitestone Pond would be nice, and he said wouldn't it just, and I said what about the Vale of Health and he said what indeed, but what he actually showed me were not the thing at all, you'd be surprised how much of Hampstead is home to the unswung cat, so I reminded him that I was after something large and comfy, with a back fence you couldn't touch from the house, after which we drove for a while and fetched up at this big brick 1930 number, very nice, I said, if crumbling, yes, said the agent, it has a lot of character all right, plus mature garden, very true, I said, the Matto Grosso suddenly seems juvenile, but I liked the house, it had that feel, and there was nothing wrong with it that a couple of international bestsellers couldn't fix, so I shook his hand and let it palm the deposit (this was 1972, remember, when things went gazump in the night) and when my wife saw it, she steadied herself on the gatepost (I say steadied, they lurched together) but she said nothing because she was eight months pregnant and would have settled for a decent manger, so it was a bit late when I strolled to the end of the street and saw this big sign that said Cricklewood.

"In a sense, yes," said the agent, when I rang, "but it is definitely Hampstead borders. Walk to the other end of the street, you're in Hampstead." "West Hampstead," I said. "Exactly," said the agent.

Very soon, I discovered how tiny Cricklewood was. Being big on the map did not signify; marketing laughed at cartography. When it was not Hampstead, Cricklewood was South Hendon, Fortune Green, Gladstone Park, Child's Hill Village, the Hocroft Estate . . . I had come to live in Shibboleth, a point never made clearer to me than when I began writing about it, and my neighbours went beserk, bombarding me with letters headed "Hampstead NW2" insisting that that was where we lived, call it Cr*****w**d and bang went property values, what was I, mad?

But Sunday changed all that. On Sunday, they were faced with shaping up or shipping out; if, that is, they could find any takers. For on Sunday, the Property Misdescriptions Act became law, and at the stroke of midnight, Cricklewood became absolutely enormous. Ask any estate agent.